ANDY GORAM
My Life

Andy Goram

My Life

with
Ken Gallacher

Virgin

First published in Great Britain in 1997 by
Virgin Books
an imprint of Virgin Publishing Ltd
332 Ladbroke Grove
London W10 5AH

A catalogue record for this book is available from the British Library.

ISBN 1 85227 691 6

Typeset by TW Typesetting, Plymouth, Devon

Printed and bound by
Mackays of Chatham, Lordswood, Chatham, Kent

Contents

Foreword – Walter Smith, Rangers Manager

It wasn't a coincidence that Andy Goram was one of my first-ever signings for Rangers. Although he certainly helped to alleviate the problem posed to the club by UEFA's decision to limit the number of 'foreign' players we could use to three, I signed him because I thought he was an outstanding goalkeeper.

When I joined the club as assistant manager to Graeme Souness, the major signings were made from England, and now here I was in 1991 – following Graeme's departure to Liverpool – with the worry of carrying too many Englishmen for our European campaigns. It was particularly daunting for me because, while I had worked closely with Graeme, this was my first managerial job and the first time I would have to make transfer decisions on my own. In Andy Goram, though, I knew I wasn't taking any chances. He had demonstrated, both at club level with Hibs and at international level with Scotland, that he was an exceptional goalkeeper. Of course, I had to sacrifice England keeper Chris Woods, but I had no qualms at all about replacing him with someone of Andy's outstanding ability. But it is not only that natural talent which has made Andy one of the finest keepers in Britain, probably in the whole of Europe. He has courage and he has honesty. When Andy makes a mistake – which isn't very often – he will own up to it. I don't think I'll ever come across such a high standard of goalkeeping over a long period of time.

I have to really think hard for examples where he has lost bad goals. There were a couple early on in his career – one in a European Cup game against Sparta Prague and another against Hearts in the Premier League at Tynecastle. But they came when he was still finding his feet at Ibrox; when he was finding out exactly what it's like to play for Rangers and just beginning to realise the extent of the demands which are made on players by the club and the supporters. The great thing about Andy was that he learned quickly – and he learned well.

Since then I can recall the one he lost at Aberdeen last season in a game where we did slip up as we headed for our ninth successive Championship, but it says a great deal for his consistency that the Pittodrie slip was being written about for days afterwards because no one could recall the last time Andy had made a similar mistake. Another goalkeeper making that kind of error would not have been subjected to the same headlines, so although Andy wouldn't take it as one, it was a back-handed compliment.

There have been times when he has come to me and accepted the blame for a goal we've lost when it hasn't even struck me that the goalkeeper was to blame. But because Andy sets himself such high standards he knows when he should get to the ball and when he has no chance of doing so – and he will never hide from the truth. If he makes a mistake – even the type of mistake which no one else notices – then he will say so. He will never apportion blame elsewhere as a way of saving himself. That's not his way. He stands up to be counted, just as he does when he is on the field and an attacker is coming through on him. I don't remember any goalkeeper being better than he is in that situation, but he has worked hard to improve his technique and continues to concentrate on that aspect of his goalkeeping. It would have been easy for Andy to rely solely on his naturally good reflexes, his timing and his eye, but he hasn't done that. He has concentrated all his efforts on the technical side of goalkeeping and that's what has made him so outstanding.

That's not to say we haven't had our differences in the six years since I signed him, however, and there was the famous occasion when I was ready to sell him. However, Andy – being Andy – reacted to the challenge which was laid in front of him and came back to play as well as ever for the team. Without a doubt, he's been one of the best signings I have made in my time as manager. The saves he has made which have won games or turned games in our favour are too many to put down on paper.

He has also overcome injury problems which would have ended the careers of other players who don't possess his strength of will. He doesn't train with the rest of the players because his injuries have made it impossible for him to do the normal work, so he does his preparations with Alan Hodgkinson, our goalkeeping coach, instead. And watching him in action, no one would notice any difference. The 'Goalie' – as he's called in the dressing room – has been an unbelievable player for the club. His contribution towards our record Championship run was both immense and immeasurable. I have never regretted signing him because he has proved himself every bit as good as I hoped he would be.

1 'Eight Was Great, Nine Was Fine, But It's Got To Be Ten In A Row'

THE TITLE OF THIS chapter is the chant which will be echoing around the grounds of Scotland throughout the coming season. We heard it at the end of last year and if ever we needed reminding – and at Rangers we don't – of the demands of the Ibrox support then we were left in no doubt as to what is required. The rollercoaster we have been on for so long isn't going to be allowed to wind down and the new players the chairman and manager Walter Smith are bringing in will have to learn very quickly that when the fans want something as badly as they want this latest target then the players are expected to deliver. I was lucky enough to be there for six of the title wins and I want to be there for more because I love the team and the fans have been really good to me.

Last season will leave an indelible imprint on the memories of thousands of Rangers supporters because it was what they had longed for. At last, Rangers had equalled the Celtic record which had stood for more than twenty years. It was set up by the Celtic teams who were managed by the legendary Jock Stein and they controlled the Scottish game from 1966 until 1974, when Rangers put an end to their run.

There were always other trophies to win but the League is the overriding goal and when we started off on our own glory run the ninth successive Championship became what everybody wanted above all else. We all knew at Ibrox how much it meant to the fans.

The last League game against Celtic at Parkhead last season was one of the biggest games we faced in all those nine seasons. It probably ranked alongside the last-day win over Aberdeen, which gave the club their third Championship in the sequence just a few months before I was bought from Hibs. Ten days earlier, Celtic had knocked us out of the Scottish Cup in the quarter-final at their ground and now they were favourites to win again. If they had, they would have been the favourites to end our title-winning run. But their players made a vital mistake after that Cup game – they got us angry. Really angry. Not only because they had beaten us and robbed us of a chance of winning the domestic treble, but also because they had gone into their famous 'huddle' after the final whistle. They have been going into that 'huddle' before games for a number of seasons now and if they think it works for them then that's fine. While we kid their players about it, none of us at Ibrox are really bothered about what they do before the game. We joke about it when we are with the Scotland team. (We have tried to persuade John Collins to tell us what the players say to each other when they get together like that, but so far to no avail.) However, going into their 'huddle' *after* the match was different. To say we didn't like it would be an understatement. We were furious, and felt as if they were ridiculing us because they had beaten us for the first time in two seasons. As we left the field their fans gave us the usual abuse – just as our support would give them – which is what we've come to expect. What we didn't expect was fellow professionals trying to belittle us. Over the next ten days, as we thought about the League game which was looming, the after-match huddle became a gnawing sore in the dressing room. And it was during these talks that we decided we would go into a huddle of our own if we got the result we wanted in that second match. I have to admit I was one of the instigators; I felt strongly about what had happened and the idea of getting our own back appealed strongly. In the event, however, I missed the game, missed being part of that important victory and missed going into the huddle in front of our dug-out at the end. However, the lads did it just as we had planned and all hell broke loose. The referee, Willie Young, ordered our players into the dressing room and mentioned the huddle in his report to the Scottish Football Association. Suddenly we were in trouble for simply doing what the Celtic players had done ten days earlier. Their then manager Tommy Burns said that we should have behaved 'with dignity' when we won the game – ironic, considering that he had said nothing about his players doing the same thing after the Cup match. It still makes little sense to me. All we were doing was having a bit of fun by celebrating the victory in the same way that the Celtic players had done before us. I still believe they only did it to annoy us and I see nothing wrong with a tit-for-tat celebration. It caused no trouble and it let our supporters know that the Celtic after-match huddle had been a motivating factor in getting the win we wanted so badly in the League match.

Despite the fuss that followed, I am still sorry I couldn't take part. If it wasn't for the knee injury I would have been in the middle of it all enjoying every moment because it was a win which will be savoured for a long time to come. It set us up for the last few games of a nine-year journey and helped make that long, long voyage a success for all of us. If you can't celebrate that kind of event, just what can you celebrate? It was the culmination of a career for so many of us and that deserved to be remembered.

The knee operation which ended the season a few weeks prematurely for me was transformed into a 'career-threatening' injury by some newspapers. The truth of the matter is that the operation was a minor one. I was in and out of hospital in 48 hours and because it was all done by a scope I don't even have a scar to show for it. The only signs are five little holes in the side of my leg. In fact, I might have been able to play in the last match of the season against Hearts at Tynecastle if the game had mattered a great deal, but of course it didn't. The Championship had been won at Tannadice a few days earlier so there was no point pushing myself back into the team when the surgeon had advised rest. A break before the end of the season and then another one in the summer was unusual for me, but it was welcome. The previous summer had seen me in the United States with Scotland for two matches at the end of the season and then on to the games in England at Euro 96 before returning to action for Rangers in Europe before our own season had begun.

Anyway, missing these games saw me described as facing an 'injury crisis', which was far from the truth. I had had one season when I was out for a considerable period of time, requiring major surgery in Los Angeles, and another season when I missed quite a number of matches through a different injury, but what people don't look at is the number of League appearances I have made in the six years I have been with Rangers. Over that period I have made 160 appearances for the first team in Premier League matches, and for a supposed 'cripple', I don't think that's too bad. That figure doesn't include League Cup, Scottish Cup, European Cup and friendly games either. Stuart McCall, who signed for the club in the same year as I did, has played in three games more but to reach that figure you have to add in the number of substitute appearances he made. Then there's David Robertson, who also joined up at Ibrox in the summer of 1991. He has played 23 games more, which is hardly a great deal considering I had almost a whole year out following the operation. In fact, during the whole nine-in-a-row saga there are only a handful of players who have made more appearances than I have, and some of them were there for longer periods. Goughie is one; John Brown another. Then there's Gary Stevens, with Coisty and Ian

Ferguson and Mark Hateley making up the rest. So I don't think I've done too badly for a crock.

It's been fascinating to see players come and go, and the past few seasons with Brian Laudrup and Paul Gascoigne have been a joy. The supporters in Scotland – not only Rangers supporters, but all supporters – have been privileged in being able to watch them in action week after week. They share the same sublime skills on the field but away from the game they are two totally different characters, Brian being so laid back and Gazza so much the opposite.

Brian likes the quiet life away from the limelight, although that's not to say that he doesn't enjoy a few beers with the lads. But family life is important to him and I think he likes the chance to unwind with his wife and children, away from the pressures which surround all the players at Ibrox at various times. Brian is such a professional and I still get as much of a kick out of watching him as any of the supporters do. He has been a terrific signing for Rangers; probably the best the gaffer has ever made, and I believe he has become a better and more effective player because he has been given the opportunity to express himself on the field. Just look at the goals he scored for us last season.

Gazza, of course, lives his life in the full glare of publicity because no one will leave him alone. I wasn't surprised when he spoke in the close season about the problems he has had just getting on with his life without being hounded by reporters and photographers. OK, he has brought some of these problems on himself – and I should know because there have been occasions when I have done the same thing – but even when he wants to go fishing he can't. That can't be right. All it does is heighten the pressure on him and people too often forget that he actually takes his job very seriously. Sure, he has his daft moments and there are times when he has behaved badly, but he's just a bubbly young kid at heart. He's extremely generous when it comes to the fans; he will always make time for them and there are numerous kind things he has done which have never been given any publicity, possibly because he doesn't court it. In the dressing room he can be really funny. If we lose a game, he will come in after the game shouting, 'It's my fault, it's my fault', and you can't help laughing because his chops go all red and he starts shaking, shouting and yelling. He takes every defeat very personally and this is just his way of getting rid of his frustrations. Winning is important to him; you have to remember that one of the reasons he gave for joining Rangers was that he wanted to win medals. He didn't have too many before he arrived and now he wants to get as many as possible. He wanted to see the Championship record equalled as much as any of the supporters.

Gazza's contribution has been immense over the two seasons he has been at the club. When he and Brian are playing together they can often be unstoppable, making it difficult for us when they have been out of the team. But when they are in place, the opposition simply don't know which one of them to mark. I'm not suggesting that they are the only guys who matter in the team but they do give us one hell of an advantage. Their consistency has been amazing. I see both of them as world-class players and I can never understand those English critics who believe that Gazza should be left out of the national side. He has the ability to open up defences which few other players possess. I watch him do it all the time. (Unfortunately, I also suffered against him at Wembley.) There is no praise high enough for the two of them in my book. When you think back to some of the great games they have played and the way Brian has tormented Celtic in the Old Firm games, you appreciate how valuable they are. There are times during games when you know that if you just play the ball to one of them, something rather special will happen. It's good to know that one run or one shot from either of these two players can turn a game – even win a game – for the team.

But there are other great Rangers players who are often overlooked and under-appreciated. I'm thinking mainly about Coisty here. He finished last season as the top scorer at the club again, yet like myself he has had to put up with people suggesting he is over the hill. It's not true. Coisty still gets goals and he is one of the best finishers I have ever seen. I used to wonder about him when I played against him; I thought there were times when he was lucky. The ball would hit off his leg, finishing up in the net, and I'd be saying, 'You lucky so-and-so'. When I got to Rangers I saw this kind of thing happen week after week, and my respect grew for him by the day. It is not luck; it is a superb positional sense inside the penalty box. Yes, he has luck as well, but if you watch him closely you will see the kind of sixth sense he has around goal. He just knows when and where the ball is going to arrive and just how he can move off his marker and score.

Coisty is seen as a bit of a Jack-the-lad, but I have witnessed him leaving Ibrox at four o'clock because he has been doing extra training and practising, even after a career with Rangers which has seen him perform in all nine Championship wins and score more goals than any other Rangers striker in history. As well as winning medal after medal, Coisty has also been able to break umpteen scoring records. He has had an incredible career and I would not bet against him scoring still more goals in the season to come. That's what he does – and he's done it better than anyone else in the country for the past decade.

It will be practically impossible to replace Goughie, not just because of his defensive skills but also because of his leadership qualities. He was a player who led by example and will carry on doing that in the States. He won't change. He will remain as professional as ever and totally single-minded. That trait brought him problems at times, including being left out of the Scotland side when he was easily the best defender around. But that's Richard. He has never been one to compromise. If you make a mistake then he won't be slow to tell you – and you accept any criticism from him because of who he is and what he has achieved in the game. We worked really hard together to get an understanding and when the pass-back rule came in we spent hours on the training ground preparing a strategy to adapt to it. We decided that we should not get too close to each other when the ball was being played through and beyond the back players. We felt it was better that I stayed as far back as possible. That meant that if a defender was forced to play the ball back to me I would have space enough and time enough to clear the ball before an attacker could reach it. That worked for us and I can only recall one occasion when we messed up. We talked it all through and went out to training to test it and while it may have looked as if I just naturally took to the new rule it wasn't like that. I probably found it easier than some keepers because I used to charge around as an outfield player in the five-a-sides at Oldham and Hibs. I think I was a frustrated centre forward back then, but having done that and played on the plastic pitch at Oldham I didn't find the adjustment too hard to make. But I do wish FIFA would stop tinkering with the rules. They are changing the pass-back one again and of course they changed the manner of taking goal kicks. All that has done is increase the opportunities for time wasting. They wanted to speed up the game and now, in a lot of cases, they have actually created a charter for time wasting. Basically they have simply made life more difficult for goalkeepers and it's hard enough without rule changes.

But the fans want success and that's what we have to try to give them. Incredibly, we have tremendous supporters all over the world – I've been to see them in Toronto, Hong Kong and Belfast. I often go over to Northern Ireland to visit the Supporters' Clubs there. They don't get to see the players very often and I enjoy meeting them all. When you are among them you realise the depth of feeling they have for Rangers and the players and exactly what success for the club has meant to them. The foreign players have all come to realise that too and those who are joining the club will soon understand the passion that the team can generate among these fans. Supporters made the journey to Russia and Vladikavkaz last season and some of the new lads could not believe it when they saw them at the hotel before the game. I doubt if any city in the world can match Glasgow in its fierce love of the game and for the rivalries which exist between the leading clubs. That's why we will be trying to win a tenth title and a new record in Scottish football; because the supporters all round the world deserve that. And that's why the players all know that while eight was great and nine was fine, it really does have to be ten in a row!

2 The Booze-Up Which Almost Ended My Rangers Career

WITHOUT A DOUBT, my years at Rangers have been the best in my career, and all the lads at the club would probably say the same. It's not just that we've had the privilege of enjoying the football and savouring the titles and cups we've won; we have also made history. In the years ahead people will look back on the successful seasons we have strung together and talk about us in the same way they talk about great players of the past at Supporters' Club functions now.

Yet I almost missed out on some of the very best of times because of my uncanny knack of hitting the self-destruct button. Anyone in the game will tell you that goalkeepers are usually a mad lot. Maybe there are odd exceptions, and I touch on that elsewhere, but it does seem to be the case that a large percentage of us end up doing things that are totally off the wall. I can't explain why. All I can say is that it's true and I qualify for membership.

This was certainly the case in the summer of 1994, when injury forced me on to the sidelines just as Rangers were winning another League Championship – their sixth in succession – and heading for the Scottish Cup Final and a possible domestic treble. I had undergone surgery the previous close season and it had been February before I returned to first-team action. Within ten games I was out again, though the injury was unconnected with the knee problem which had taken me to California for an operation.

The new blow came up at Tannadice in a League game against Dundee United which we drew 0-0, and it affected my other leg – or at least, the other hip. It may have been that I was trying to favour that side as opposed to the one which had been weakened a little by the surgery – I had been warned that this was a possibility. Whatever the reason, the injury was caused by kicking the ball out, something which puts extra pressure on goalkeepers following the alteration to the pass-back rule.

So there I was, my comeback plans placed on sudden hold after just reaching full fitness again, both physically and mentally. The Scottish Cup semi-final against Kilmarnock was less than a week off and I knew I was out of that. If Rangers went through, the final loomed seven weeks ahead (and of course we did get through, although it took a replay to decide that we would play Dundee United in the May final).

The club hoped I would be fit to play in the final but I had nagging doubts and never really believed I would be ready in time for the Hampden game. The operation, the long lay-off and then this set-back had knocked a huge dent in my confidence and I couldn't see a recovery taking place in time.

Maybe it was the worries over my fitness gnawing away at me which caused all the problems which were to follow – the problems which saw me slapped on the transfer list, facing a future away from Rangers Football Club. And that was something which, quite frankly, frightened me to death.

I had spent so many seasons dreaming of a move to Rangers that the idea of leaving was something I just couldn't contemplate. Rangers was the ultimate for me. I had spent all those years at Oldham learning my trade and then another few seasons with Hibs, trying to establish myself as one of the leading goalkeepers in Scotland, and finally I got what I wanted. I was playing for the top club in the country, one of the best clubs in Britain and a team which was recognised all across Europe as well. Risking that must be the most stupid thing I've ever done. The roots of the trouble, though, lay with the kernel of doubt which continually thrust its way into my thoughts as I rested the damaged hip which was causing me so much grief.

Every time I felt a twinge of pain it was as if the injury was sending me a message: 'You've no chance of playing against Dundee United. Just forget it. Think about next season. Concentrate on being fit by then.'

I suppose I was talking myself out of playing in the final but even now I can understand why I was adopting that attitude. The shock of the close-season operation, the severity of the surgery and the long, long months spent in recovery had taken their toll. I just thought it was too much to expect me to be fit as quickly as the club wanted. I thought I was an expert on injuries by this time.

However, the real experts – the medical people at Ibrox – were not thinking along the same lines as I was. They were taking a much more positive view. They wanted me to be fit and ready, and in goal in the game at Hampden. It was this disagreement between myself and the back-room staff at the club which eventually brought the confrontation with Rangers manager Walter Smith and almost saw me packing my bags and leaving the club.

So there I was in that soccer no man's land where long-term injuries leave you suffering, and it was only a few weeks away from the final. That's when the gaffer suggested that I should go off on a short holiday with the family – to soak up a bit of sun and rest the leg. After all, I couldn't do any work at Ibrox. I couldn't train and I'd been told that rest rather than treatment was what was needed. The manager felt that relaxing somewhere in the sun would be better than moping around Ibrox feeling sorry for myself and looking more and more miserable by the day.

It did seem a good idea at the time.

My wife, Tracy, agreed that it was the kind of break I needed, so we made the arrangements and Tracy's mum and dad agreed to come with us to help look after our son Lewis – who was a bit of a handful then and I was obviously in no shape to run around a beach after him. We booked an apartment in Tenerife, little knowing that a whole lot of trouble was just around the corner.

The first few days of the week-long holiday went extremely well. The sun shone, I got the rest the gaffer and the doctors had advised, and although I still wasn't convinced that I would be able to play in the final I had to admit that I felt better.

Any player will tell you that there's nothing worse than hanging around the dressing rooms when you're injured. It's so depressing when everyone else is preparing for the game and you're not involved. So to be away from that and detached from it, you're able to look at things a little more rationally. In that sense, the mental sense, the break had worked. In a physical sense, I didn't believe it had made any difference to the damaged hip.

That's what eventually got me in bother. On the second to last day of the holiday, we were all walking back up from the beach when I looked across at a pavement cafe and to my amazement saw Joe Royle, my old manager at Oldham, having a drink with some of the players I had known when I'd been down there. There were champagne bottles littered all over the tables and it turned out that Joe had taken the players away for a consolation break after having been relegated from the old First Division.

That's the kind of manager Joe was – a great lad and someone who really thinks about his players. This gesture was typical of him. All the lads were there, including Mike Milligan, who'd been a mate of mine at Boundary Park. Inevitably they asked me to join them and just as inevitably I agreed. I hadn't seen them in ages and this was a chance to catch up on all the gossip. I told Tracy and her folks that I would have a couple of drinks and see them back at the apartment a bit later on. How late I didn't realise. Perhaps drinking champagne and peach schnapps – Bellinis I think they're called – in a near 100 degrees heat wasn't the best idea in the world, but it was good to have a laugh with the lads and I really enjoyed myself. I'd always been close to Joe, and still am, and have never forgotten that when I was just a kid at Oldham he gave me my chance, encouraged me and handed out a lot of good advice.

The following day was our last day on the island – our flight home was at five o'clock the next morning. As usual we headed down to the beach, only this time I didn't make it there. En route I heard a shout of 'Goalie' – and there was Graeme Sharp and some of the other players having a few beers in a bar. Again they asked me to join them and again I said OK. Promising to join them a bit later, Tracy, her mum and dad and Lewis carried on to the beach without me. Some four or five hours later they found me in the bar, still drinking. I suspect Tracy knew that I wouldn't make the beach because I'm not a great one for lying around doing nothing, and I'd had my fill of that in the five or six days beforehand. This time I told her I'd be up at the apartment in half an hour. We'd planned to have our last meal together and then pack for the early-morning flight back to Edinburgh.

The lads then decided it was time to move on to another venue, where they were going to meet up with the rest of the Oldham squad. Needless to say, I went along with them, still intending to join Tracy and the others when I said I would. Around six or seven o'clock I started to say my farewells, which inevitably were only greeted with a lot of stick. It was the old 'man or a mouse' bit, and guess who fell for it?

We went on to another few bars, and one drink led to

several more, and the next thing I remember is waking up in Mike Milligan's room. It was one o'clock – I only had a few hours to get back to the apartment and get to the airport. And then I realised that it was one o'clock in the afternoon. There I was, eight hours after my flight for home had gone, stranded without a passport or clothes, except the T-shirt and shorts I was wearing to go down to the beach the previous morning. It was like a bad dream.

My wallet was also considerably lighter than it had been and I certainly didn't have enough for an air ticket home. I was in big trouble. My immediate thought was that I would get hell from Tracy. The next one was how on earth I was ever going to get home to get the expected tongue-lashing. I didn't have an answer to that one.

My solution was to get up and go and have lunch with the Oldham lads and then head on down to the beach with them and have a game of football. Even though I couldn't move much I was able to stand in goal. While I was doing so, I thought about the mess I'd got myself in. No air ticket. No passport. No clothes. Only forty quid left. Frightened to phone home. I knew I wasn't due back at Ibrox for another week but I was terrified of speaking to Tracy. I'm not a person who enjoys confrontation. I don't mind it when Tracy dishes out the silent treatment but I can't handle a really major row, and this was what I was headed for – if I ever got home.

I phoned a friend in Edinburgh the next day and asked him if he could organise something through a travel agent to get me back home. He arranged for a ticket and some money to be waiting for me. He was also able to arrange things so that I could get back home without my passport – something which had been causing me a great deal of worry. Then I borrowed some clothes from one of Joe's mates – things were looking up.

That, however, just added to my problems. Unfortunately, whenever I see that troubles are clearing up, I take that as a signal to drop back into my 'men behaving badly' mode. I had clothes to wear, money in my pocket and an air ticket for a flight home in 36 hours. All was right with the world – except that with time to spare and money to spend the party with the Oldham players simply started up again.

Only this time there was another complication – which thankfully I had been warned of by my mate in Edinburgh. Somehow the tabloids had got hold of a story from somewhere that I had gone walkabout on the island and they were sending out a news team to get details of this 'Carry On in the Canaries'. It was all I needed. Instead of lying low, however, which I should have done, I continued to frequent the restaurants, cafes and bars around where we were staying.

What saved me were two bouncers who happened to be Rangers supporters. When the newsmen arrived – one of them with all his camera equipment hanging round his neck – they sent them off on a wild goose chase. But I knew that would only save me for so long, and when these two 'reporters' sent some story back home saying I had been in a brawl I knew I had to return to Scotland as soon as possible.

Even that didn't turn out to be as simple as it should have been because they turned up at the airport looking for me. I had to spend two hours sitting in the toilets until the coast was clear and I somehow managed to board the flight back to Edinburgh without the press seeing me.

Not that that stopped them writing about me, which didn't help my case in the long run. I received the expected welcome from Tracy, although I think she understood that the worry over the injury had been niggling away at me. Back at Ibrox, after questioning me about Tenerife, the gaffer asked me if I felt fit enough to play in the final. I said no, explaining that I had never really expected to be able to, and so I wasn't even named in the pool of players for Hampden.

Unfortunately we lost the game 1-0. Even more unfortunately for me, the goal we lost came after a misunderstanding between my deputy Ally Maxwell and defender Dave McPherson. It didn't help that afterwards people were saying that if I had been in goal then the crucial mistake would not have been made and we would have been celebrating back-to-back trebles. But we still had reasons to enjoy ourselves that night because we had won yet another Championship and the League Cup – and we'd been in the Scottish Cup Final. Not a bad season at all.

Most of the lads seemed to look on the bright side too. It was a good night and the disappointment of the afternoon was forgotten as the better times were remembered. In fact, considering we had lost to the Tannadice team, it was one of the best nights I can remember. There was just something which seemed to gel. The rapport between the players has always been special and it was there that night. You could feel it in the air.

Then, towards the end of the night, came the bombshell. The first-team coach David Dodds informed me that the manager wanted to see me at Ibrox at ten o'clock on Monday morning. I didn't know what it was about, but I knew it wasn't good news.

At first I thought it had to do with the end-of-season trip which the players had organised as part of Ally McCoist's testimonial year. One of the dinners was being held in Toronto and a whole bunch of us had agreed to go with Coisty and make it a pretty special event for the big Canadian support Rangers have over there. In the wake of the Tenerife business, I thought the gaffer had probably decided that I'd had enough breaks to last me for some time and was going to ban me from the Toronto trip. That was, quite honestly, the worst-case scenario that I could envisage that Saturday night. I was hoping that I was wrong – but not in the way I was eventually proved wrong.

I arrived at Ibrox at quarter to ten on the Monday. Some of the other players were around but not too many of the first-team squad. Basically, the lads who were there were the ones who were being given free transfers or being placed on the transfer list, either because their contracts were up or because they hadn't been able to reach the standards which Rangers set for all their players. Needless to say, it wasn't the happiest of occasions – here were youngsters whose dreams were over. Most of them asked me what I was doing there but of course I had no idea. It didn't once cross my mind that I might finish up in the same boat as them; leaving Rangers and searching for another club which would never, ever match up.

Just before ten o'clock I started to make my way along the corridor towards the main foyer. I knew by now that the gaffer was treating this seriously because he was in his upstairs office – and when you went there it was never for good news. The players always dread going up the 'marbles' – meaning the marble staircase which dominates the front hall at the stadium. If you were called into the downstairs office, where the coaching staff change for training, then it was never for any major offence. But the 'marbles' meant trouble.

On the way I saw Davie Dodds and I can remember saying to him, 'Doddsy, he's not going to let me go to Canada, is he?', because that was still what I guessed was going to happen at the face to face. Doddsy didn't say anything and just walked on, shaking his head. I took that to be confirmation that the next morning, when Coisty and co. went off to Canada, I would be sitting at home as a punishment.

It was a deadpan face that greeted me when I knocked on the door to the manager's office. As I walked in I noticed how intimidating the office is and how threatening the big desk and manager's chair looked. All around the walls are photographs of previous managers of the club – not too many of them when you consider that Rangers

Football Club is now almost 125 years old, but enough to strike the fear of death into you when you are summoned to a meeting with the gaffer.

It was the gaffer's idea, apparently, to have them all hanging there as a reminder of the club's history: the first manager William Wilton and then Bill Struth, Scot Symon, Davie White, Willie Waddell, Jock Wallace, John Greig and Graeme Souness. As you sit down it's as if all of them are looking at you with something less than approval.

It was in that atmosphere that I waited to hear the verdict – and I didn't have to wait too long. He simply turned round and told me quite simply and starkly: 'I'm putting you on the transfer list.' That was it. Straight to the point. I was left wondering if this was one of his wind-ups. On many occasions he's been known to say something really harsh or tell you something really serious with a completely expressionless face. Then, within ten seconds or so, his face will alter and you realise that he's been having you on. And that's what I thought was happening to me.

Here we go, I thought. In a minute he'll tell me I'm not going to Toronto and it will seem as if I'm getting off lightly. I was so sure of that – so sure that he couldn't mean what he had just said – that I felt myself starting to smirk, and there was even the feeling that I might start to snigger. I mean, how could he possibly put me up for sale? I was the international goalkeeper. I was an important member of his first-team squad. I was an automatic choice for the Rangers first team when I was fit.

This was all going through my mind when he repeated his first statement: 'I'm putting you on the list.' Again he said it with that deadpan look and this time it sunk in. He meant it. There were no smiles. This was for real. He hadn't been winding me up at all. My career with Rangers looked as if it was coming to an end. I tried to grasp all of that and managed to blurt out, 'Why?' He answered me without the slightest hesitation.

'As far as I'm concerned,' he told me, 'you didn't make a big enough effort to get yourself fit in time for the Scottish Cup Final. So I'm getting rid of you. That's it.'

Even then I found it difficult to grasp. I knew that I *had* messed him around and that I *had* screwed up royally when the club sent me to Tenerife to rest and recuperate. I also knew that I was probably a stone overweight because I hadn't been able to train. But I also knew I could sort things out.

All I could think about was being able to stay at Ibrox. Nothing else mattered. 'Why are you doing this to me now?' I asked. 'Can you not wait until the start of the season when I've had the whole of the summer to train and lose weight and get myself back to proper fitness before you make a decision? If I report back for pre-season training and I'm not in decent shape then I'll hold up my hands and you can sell me. Just don't do it now.'

But there was no moving him. He just looked at me, shook his head and said, 'Look, I've made my decision now. I don't want to have to do this but I've got to do it. It's not a personal decision. This is a footballing decision and I have to have that side of things right and I have to think about the good of the club. That's what has influenced me to do what I have done this morning.'

I knew I couldn't argue my case because I could feel tears welling up behind my eyes. He knew he'd hurt me but I didn't want him to see just how much. At that moment I just wanted to get away on my own; to get out of that office away from Walter and the accusing glare of each Rangers manager. I felt more humiliated than I had ever felt in my whole life.

Even now it's hard for me to think back to those few minutes in the manager's office because I am reminded of how close I came to wrecking my Rangers career. I didn't know then what I was going to do, but I did have one question to ask. As I was going out the door, I asked if I could go to Toronto.

He looked at me, shrugged and said, 'Do what you like.'

I headed for the referee's room and just sat there for half an hour on my own. Still very upset, I was clinging to the hope that this was a monumental kick up the backside and all Walter was doing was putting the frighteners on me so that I would respond in the right way. That was my only hope and I sat there trying to get to grips with the whole thing. I went round and round in circles but kept returning to that one – that the gaffer didn't mean it and would change his mind.

Somehow, though, deep down, I think I knew that he had meant what he said. I was nothing more than a memory now and he would be looking for a goalkeeper to replace me. All the hard work I had put in – all the years of apprenticeship at Oldham and then at Hibs – had gone down the drain. This was the end of all my dreams and it was all down to my own stupidity.

I telephoned Tracy to tell her and discovered that Walter had spoken to her on the Saturday night at the party and prepared her for the worst but sworn her to secrecy. He had not wanted Tracy to hear the news from anyone else, especially a reporter, and even in my despair I appreciated this courtesy. That was some kind of confirmation for me that the 'For Sale' sign was official.

After talking to Tracy I went along to the dressing room and found that some of the first-team squad were in, having treatment or doing a bit of training. Ian Durrant, Ally McCoist and John Brown were there and saw straight away that something was wrong. But it wasn't until I told them that they realised just how serious it was.

At first they didn't believe me. They were as stunned as I had been, and Coisty and Durranty suggested that we go for a drink in town and talk the whole thing through. They were convinced that it was a warning from the gaffer – a shot across the bows to let me know that Rangers would not tolerate the kind of behaviour I had been guilty of while on holiday.

When we got into town the newspaper bills were already out. ''Gers sack Goram' roared at me from every street corner. That's what finally brought it home to me. I suddenly realised that this was happening, that it was all genuine, every last bit of it. Making it so immediately public meant that Walter was not about to change his mind. The other lads kept telling me that it was only a kick up the backside, that it would all blow over during the close season and that everything would be back to normal when I reported for training, but by this time I was past clutching at straws. Even as they all tried to cheer me up I knew in my heart of hearts that Rangers were going to sell me. It was the end of the road for me and the team I loved.

I decided, rightly or wrongly, that I would go to Toronto the following day. One of the thoughts uppermost in my mind by then was the fact that the newspapers would be tailing me, looking for reasons, and I just didn't want to face the kind of questioning I knew they would put me through. By getting out of the way I would escape all of that and possibly allow the whole affair to settle down a little bit. It wasn't as simple as that, of course, because the newspapers sent reporters to Toronto. A few of the Glasgow-based writers were in Hamilton, Ontario, covering a tournament which involved Celtic, and they were sent to search for me. Fortunately they didn't reach me and I was able to relax a little and think about what might come next.

It was an ideal time to let our hair down but my heart wasn't in it. I couldn't forget that this would be the last time I would ever enjoy the camaraderie of the first-team squad, which had become so important to me in the few years I had been with Rangers. There is a real bond between the players which has so often helped us through difficult games and hard times. Now it was going to be snatched away from me, and while I attempted to put a brave face on things for the supporters over there I felt increasingly miserable as the days slipped past. I hated the idea of going home and facing up to an uncertain future.

It was in one of my dark moments that 'Bomber' – John Brown, now the reserve-team coach at Ibrox – pulled me aside. 'What do you think you're playing at?' he asked. None of the players wanted me to leave, he told me. They wanted me to be there again next season, back in goal and fully fit for the new season. Then he warned me that I would have to work really hard during the summer and that by the time pre-season training started I would have to be a whole lot fitter than I was at that moment.

'If you knuckle down and work hard while you're on holiday – and get rid of the extra weight – you have a chance. But you have to lose weight and you have to do that before coming back to Ibrox. If you do that, really show willing, then everything will work out OK. But if you look as if you're not bothering your backside then he'll sell you just as quickly as he can.'

Basically Bomber was spelling out to me what I already knew deep down. It was in my own hands to some extent. I could continue to feel sorry for myself – and I was doing a bit too much of that – or I could get on with my career. There was a choice there for me and it was plain enough. I could spend my holiday as I had spent my last and do nothing to improve my levels of fitness then find myself transferred to some other club, or I could dust myself down, pick myself up and start all over again – at my fighting weight! Bomber wasn't really telling me anything I didn't know but I needed his words of advice to reinforce my own beliefs. It meant a lot when he took me aside like that. He was one of the senior professionals at the club and he was part of the best defensive set-up I have ever played in – Dave McPherson at right back, Richard Gough and Bomber in the middle and Dave Robertson on the left – which gave him added stature in my book. Now here he was taking time off to tell me that I shouldn't give up without a fight. Coisty said more or less the same thing and Durranty pitched in his views, and gradually I came to realise that I had to get myself back in shape. It was the only way left for me.

Thinking about what was required and actually disciplining myself to do it was different, of course. I wasn't able to go on any of the long runs along the beach with the other players; that was out as far as I was concerned. I never had been the best long-distance runner in the world but the surgeon in Los Angeles who had operated on my knee had warned me against that kind of exercise. The wear and tear on my damaged knee would have finished me – I wouldn't have lasted more than a couple of seasons if I attempted that route back to fitness. So I had to find another way.

Diet became important. I spent the whole time eating grilled fish and salad. I weighed myself almost every day and soon knew that I would be OK when I reported back to Ibrox on that first day. The training staff have a note of the weight that every player should be when they return after the holiday and they check that on a weekly basis during the season. This time I reported in under the required weight and had actually shed a stone during the summer weeks. To my relief, the manager included me in the group of players who were going to the training camp Rangers have used in Italy for a number of years now. It's there at Il Ciocco that the gruelling pre-season work is done, but I couldn't join in all of the sessions because of my knee. Even at home when the season is progressing, I only train a couple of days a week because I have to be very careful. What I could do was concentrate on my diet – which was simple enough to do at Il Ciocco because the people who run the place are accustomed to dealing with professional footballers – and swim as much as possible in the pool.

Whenever I could join in with the rest of the lads I did, and I played in the practice games which helped tone me up. In fact, things went so well and I felt so much better that I started to wonder which major clubs might be interested in me. But I knew that no club could ever beat Rangers in my book, and that's what kept hurting me more than anything else as I tried to come to terms with a situation which found me in limbo.

Walter hadn't said anything to me at all other than the curt acknowledgement that I had passed the weight test when I reported back. After that I was just treated the same way as everyone else in the squad, although I knew they were in a very different position to the one I was in. They knew their future with Rangers was assured – and I did not. All I could do was keep working, keep the weight down and toe the line. John Brown's advice in Toronto kept coming back to mind and I knew he was right.

The one thing I felt was going in my favour was that Rangers did not appear to have made a move for any other goalkeeper during the summer. There is never any shortage of players who would jump at the chance of coming to Ibrox so that gave me hope. It looked like I would still be playing for a while at least. We had an important qualifying game looming in Europe at the start of the 1994–95 season, when we had to face AEK Athens, with the winners of the home and away tie going through to the Champions' League. Before that, of course, there were other matches, which I played in. I then found myself in the squad for Athens and it was there I learnt that I had been reprieved.

The gaffer had still said nothing. Leaving me to sweat, I suppose; watching and waiting to see how I had responded to the warning he had given me. Then in the Greek capital, a day or two before the game, he approached me in the hotel and said quietly, 'You're off the list from now.' Those were the sweetest words I have ever heard. All the agonies I had gone through and all the worries which had haunted me through the close season, gnawing away day after day, suddenly vanished.

I was a Rangers player again. I was still one of the lads. I wasn't going to be sold because I had been able to convince the manager that I could and would still do a job for the club. My fitness had returned and now my confidence surged back too.

Interestingly, I have never blamed Walter Smith for a minute. I knew I had been totally to blame and felt extremely guilty, although in my defence I still believe that I would never have been able to play in that Cup Final. But that was not the manager's view and he had the right to see me as physically fit as possible before that match. When he didn't get that he was entitled to take the action he did. I was overweight and unfit and I could have no complaints over what he did. At the time I wondered if the other players had been right; that he had simply gone through the whole exercise in an effort to bring me to my senses, and for a spell I thought that was probably the case. Last season, however, more than two years further on down the line, I asked him about it.

We were both in London in February 1997 to watch the England v Italy World Cup game and we met up for a meal in Langan's before heading out to Wembley. The assistant manager Archie Knox was also there, and after we had eaten I asked Walter if he *had* meant it when he threatened to place me on the transfer list. He just looked at me and said, 'Yes'. I knew then that if I hadn't listened to Bomber that day, I would not have been sitting there in London with the gaffer. He had meant it all right. That morning in his office at Ibrox he was ready to sell me to any club who showed an interest in buying me. We had a laugh about it in Langan's that day but I have never forgotten that fateful morning. And I am always aware that if my standards drop below what Rangers and the manager expect I'll probably be out of Ibrox before my feet touch the ground.

It is not a theory I have ever wanted to test. When it comes to protecting the interests of Rangers Football Club, Walter Smith will always stand firm. The club comes first with him and little else matters.

3 Troubles With Scotland

THERE DOESN'T SEEM to be any argument about it: I attract controversy. It's not just with Rangers, either, and not just off the field, because I've had my share of troubles with the national team too. This has never been more true than during the qualifying matches for the European Championship in England in the summer of 1996 when one weekend I suddenly found myself as Public Enemy Number One all round the country.

My patriotism was called into question and there were people who even tagged me a traitor. And most of them added that I should never play for Scotland again – and all because I called off from a qualifying game against Finland at Hampden.

No one would really listen to my explanation at the time. I was hung out to dry by most of the media when in reality all I was attempting to do was make sure that I didn't let my country down in an important game. It was difficult for me to accept that kind of criticism but I should have known that the only people who could understand what was going through my mind were other professional footballers, particularly goalkeepers. We are, after all, a breed apart. There are occasions when only another goalkeeper is able to appreciate the problems which can be thrown up in advance of a major game or the reasons for mistakes which are made during games.

You try to confide in others and explain how important it is to be focused solely on what is happening out there on the field, or attempt to guide them through the split-second decision-making process that all keepers go through in games, and their eyes glaze over. Nobody else can identify with the very special worries we have. So it was all too easy for the media when Scotland manager Craig Brown told them at a press conference that I was not 'mentally attuned' to play in the game which was vital for Scotland as we aimed to qualify for the finals of Euro 96. They saw that Rangers had a European Cup preliminary round match against Anorthosis of Cyprus the week after the Finnish game and they knew that these games were crucial for the club and brought massive bonuses for the players who took part. The money which the chairman, David Murray, makes available to the players who take part in the two games is way ahead of most of the bonuses we collect during the remainder of the year. If you play in the games and help the club to qualify for the later stages of the tournament in the Champions' League format then you can expect to have around £25,000 to £30,000 extra in your salary. The reward is high because the riches awaiting the club can soar to around £5 million for the three group games, and then even more if you reach the quarter-finals. There is also the challenge involved. These are the games which matter to every player. The European Cup – and especially the Champions' League – is the biggest stage of all for club football. As a club we have made it to the League set-up on three occasions and twice have faced major disappointments. These are dealt with elsewhere in the book but it's still important to remember that we *have* reached that top level where you are playing against the very elite of European football. And at least once we were unlucky not to reach the tournament final.

But back to the game against Finland. It was all too easy for the critics to hammer me because they chose to believe that the money on offer for the games in Cyprus mattered more to me than playing for Scotland. It was a simple explanation for the much more involved and complicated situation in which I found myself and very few of them were ready to lend me a sympathetic ear. I was the villain of the week; the greedy footballer who put money ahead of playing for the national side; the guy with the English accent who maybe should never have been chosen to play for Scotland in the first place. After all, ran that argument, he was born in England, wasn't he? It didn't matter that all my family roots had been in Scotland; that in the house when I was growing up we always supported Scotland when they were playing England in the annual match. In fact, we supported Scotland in everything! And until that Saturday morning when my decision not to play was made public, my birthplace and my accent had never been thrown in my face by anyone.

To his great credit, and I remain indebted to him for his support to this day, Craig Brown stood by me. It would have been very easy for him to join the bandwagon the media had set rolling and announce that I would not be considered for any of his squads in the future. He was, after all, under enormous pressure at the time. This match against Finland and another upcoming home game against Greece – the one team who had beaten us so far in the group matches – would decide whether or not we travelled across the Border to England the next summer. A great deal was at stake for Brown, the players and the entire nation. I don't suppose he really needed to have my problems suddenly rear up into massive controversy.

However, Craig did not let that influence his feelings towards me. He was disappointed and a bit stunned, I think, when I first told him. I had reported to Hampden at the same time as the other players but I had not taken any training gear with me because for the previous few days I had mulled the issue over in my mind and come to the conclusion I would not be able to concentrate 100 per cent on the international match if I was selected to play against the Finns. I explained to Craig what was going through my mind and I could see that he was trying to understand where I was coming from. It clearly wasn't easy for him and at first he tried to talk me into staying with the squad of players, going to the pre-match headquarters, training with the rest of the lads, working with the other goalkeepers and generally living with them during the build-up to the game and then seeing how I felt after 48 hours. I said no.

I appreciated what Craig was trying to do; he probably thought that merely being with the rest of the international players would help change my mind. Or, at the very least, if I stayed around then the publicity – and all of it was going to be adverse – could be controlled a little if not deflected completely.

However, I knew that nothing was going to change my mind. I told Craig that I had serious concerns about taking part in the game and I explained my reasons to him in as much detail as I could. Yes, there was the thought of the European Cup game against Anorthosis and all that meant to my club, and it was there in my mind and affecting my current judgements. But there was also the memory of being injured the previous season when I played for Scotland in Athens when I'd been taken off and left to face the wreckage of the rest of my season with Rangers. All of that was churning through my mind; all of it totally wiping out the thought of playing in the Finnish game and the preparations which would be necessary for that. There was just no way that I could concentrate and by this time I had convinced myself of this. There was no going back now.

I had simply switched off from the Finland international and moved my mind on to what I had to do for my club. That may sound strange but it's often the way when you're a goalkeeper. You hype yourself up for a game and that's all that matters to you. I'm sure others are the same as me. While he obviously wanted me to play for Scotland, my goalkeeping coach Alan Hodgkinson understood the position I was in. It was difficult for Hodgy. He was caught between everyone. He was coaching me with Rangers and he was on the Scotland backroom staff as well, so he had to take a step back from it all and then give his views. Like Craig, he wanted me to stay with the squad and be available to play if selected – which seemed likely – but he also understood my predicament.

The trouble I brought on myself was unbelievable but I still felt that I had to be honest and up front. It would have been a whole lot worse if I had gone into the game with my mind elsewhere and given away a soft goal! That was my fear; that was what concerned me most. I was frightened that I would go on to the field in what was a crucial European Championship qualifying game and let everyone down. The other players. The manager and his backroom staff. The supporters from all around the country who were so desperate for us to reach the finals because, after all, they were being played just across the Border in England.

I didn't want to take the chance. Hodgy always preached to me that I had to be 100 per cent focused when I was going into any game and if I wasn't then I would surely mess up. That's what I feared I might do and so I thought it would be better to come out before the game, say my piece and take the stick rather than contribute to a Scottish defeat. I still think that was the right thing to do even though the knives were out for me and remained out for a long, long time afterwards. I suffered but it was still better than being crucified for losing a goal and it was deeply embedded in my mind that that was exactly what I would do.

I would have been cheating an awful lot of people if I had stayed silent and then gone on to the field without being properly prepared mentally. I spelled all of that out to Craig and eventually he agreed that there was little point in my hanging around if I wasn't going to be considered for the game. He took it a lot better than I had expected because, after all, he had a different set of priorities. He had a game to win and he wanted his strongest squad of players to be with him in the preparation period. And there I was, offering him nothing more than a muddled response to his questions. Perhaps it was because I found it so difficult to explain it all to him that he realised that I *did* have a problem. Whatever he thought, he must have come to the conclusion that it would be a dangerous risk to play me if I didn't want to be in the team.

It wasn't an easy meeting for either of us. Eventually we did reach some kind of understanding and he seemed to comprehend that these worries were all-consuming and making it impossible for me to do my job as a goalkeeper the following week. I also needed to stress that I still wanted to be a part of the European Championship group of players – if my club form was good enough. There was no way that I wanted to walk off into the international wilderness over this affair. I wanted to be back involved with Scotland when my mind was clear and there was nothing which could divert me from the job of keeping goal for the international team.

This was a one-off, I explained, and it would not happen again.

Or, at least, it was highly unlikely it would ever happen again.

Of course, I knew that while Craig might select me for the squad again there was no guarantee that I would be in the team. That was the risk I was taking. I knew how well Jim Leighton was playing with Hibs. He had been the man in possession for most of the previous season when I had been out through injury and he had played superbly. But that was a gamble I was willing to take. What I refused to do was gamble with Scotland's European dreams and I knew that with Jim there I wouldn't be doing that.

In fact, who's to say that I would have been first choice for that game? The way Jim had performed, particularly in the drawn game in Moscow which had been one of the best results the team achieved, he might well have been ahead of me and I wouldn't have had any right to quibble about that decision.

It would have been much easier for me to say that I was not 100 per cent fit. With my medical history no one would have thought that that was anything at all unusual, but I felt, rightly or wrongly, that it was better to tell the truth. In any case, during a previous World Cup campaign, the Scotland manager at the time, Andy Roxburgh, had claimed that Rangers' games against Leeds United in the European Cup had overshadowed the Scotland matches and that the national team had suffered as a result. That had some relevance to my own position. If a major club game had affected the World Cup team in a previous season then it could affect an individual – yours truly – on this occasion. Jim Leighton and I had been together for ten years at this stage and I knew that he would be able to sympathise with what was going on in my mind and play against Finland without upsetting the team in any way whatsoever. After all, this was the man who had the record number of caps for a Scotland goalkeeper and he'd been through a heap of worries himself in his career.

When I look back at the World Cup Finals in Italy in 1990 I can remember thinking that I might be playing instead of Jim because of what had happened to him at Manchester United. That was an awful time for him, though only Jim could know the real, gut-wrenching pain he must have felt when he was dropped by United's manager Alex Ferguson from the FA Cup Final replay just weeks before we went off to prepare for the World Cup.

Les Sealey took his place in the replay when United won the Cup and when Jim joined the Scotland squad he was really down. It must have been a huge blow because it was

Fergie who had taken him south to shore up a defence which was never as well organised as the one he had had at Aberdeen. The Pittodrie team – and Scotland for that matter – had Willie Miller and Alex McLeish together playing in front of Jim. There was a special understanding between these three, something almost psychic. So when Jim first moved south he must have wondered what he had gone into. It was far from being the same at United and Jim was asked to shoulder a lot of responsibility. It didn't matter who was going to be in goal at that stage of Fergie's team building; he was always going to have problems because of the lack of organisation immediately in front of goal.

When the axe fell at that most critical of times, it was Jim who got it, and an awful lot of people didn't know if he would recover from the psychological blow he had been handed. But Jim had a toughness and a resilience which carried him through the initial period and sustained him later on too.

Ironically, the press were on my side in Italy and wanted me to play. Deep down, though, I did not see that Jim being axed by Manchester United would affect Andy Roxburgh's thinking as regards the national team. Also, having Alan Hodgkinson there with Scotland – he was also Jim's club coach at Manchester United – seemed to me to stack the odds in his favour. I wasn't yet working with Alan at club level so he knew Jim much better. He would know if Jim had recovered his confidence enough to play against Costa Rica in our opening game in Genoa. Still, while I had doubts, the pressure from the media did make me think that I might get the number one spot. And when I didn't it hit me quite hard.

I remember how it happened. Andy Roxburgh didn't call us together and make any big deal out of it. Nor did he just call the goalkeepers in and tell them the position before he made it public. It just came out at a normal team meeting. There was no big, dramatic meeting when the manager and Jim and myself fell out spectacularly over the decision. It's never like that, but this time it was so far away from that scenario that I find it hard to believe myself.

We were called to a tactics talk in the conference room which had been set aside for us in the Bristol Hotel in Rapallo, our headquarters for our first two games in Genoa against Costa Rica and Sweden. The way Andy worked was by having separate meetings for each area of the team. So the goalkeepers and the defenders were in one session, then the midfield players and then the at- tackers. In this way he was able to fully explain the roles of the different players and stress just how they were expected to play together. After these meetings, everyone was then called together as the tactics for the games were laid out. On this particular occasion, the talk was maybe two or three days before the opening match, and the three keepers – Jim, Bryan Gunn and myself – were there with the defensive players as Andy took out the tactics board and began placing the markers on it as he talked about the system he was intending to use.

When he got to the goalkeeping marker he just said that Jim would be playing and his decision had been based on the experience that he had had in the World Cup finals before. He didn't even pause to let it sink in or look up to see if there had been any reaction. He just moved on to the back four and began to name them.

That's how he broke the news that I wasn't going to play in the Italy finals. I don't really remember what was said at the rest of the team talk. I sometimes try to think back but there's nothing there. It's as if I simply shut off when I heard that I was out and Jim was going to play – almost as if I said to myself that all of this had nothing to do with me any longer. As we left the room, Jim shook my hand and said 'Sorry' and I like to think I would have done the same. In fact, I think I did do it subsequently when things went my way. Thankfully, it made no difference to our relationship. Our friendship is too strong to be disturbed because of a team selection. After all, we both know that only one of us can play in these games. But that doesn't soften the blow when you find out you're not playing.

In retrospect, Andy Roxburgh made the right decision. Jim had been damaged by the Cup Final replay blow but he was able to come back stronger than ever before. He was probably a better man for that experience though no one would want to have to go through what he did. In some ways it became a part of the learning process for him and when he had further troubles at club level he had the will to battle on and mount what was an astonishing comeback. I might have been disappointed at the time but my admiration for Jim Leighton grew then and has continued to grow ever since.

I was rooting for him in those games in Italy just as I knew he would have been rooting for me if the roles had been reversed. During the tournaments we live together and work together – and we celebrate or suffer together. Above all, we stay mates.

We went through the same thing when it came to the European Championship finals in England in the summer of 1996. Four years earlier I had been in goal for the Euro matches in Sweden – the first time Scotland had ever qualified for the finals – but at that time Jim was going through a bad patch at club level and it was Gordon Marshall of Celtic who was the recognised number two keeper.

For England, though, Jim's renaissance was complete. He was now with Hibs, his confidence was back and his professionalism had not been affected by the tough times he had been forced to endure at Manchester United and Dundee. He had also played in more of the qualifying games than I had done – mostly because of my injury problems – and my failure to play against Finland still went against me in some quarters.

As the finals loomed closer and closer, the debate over the goalkeeping position became more and more intense. When we went to America right at the end of the season Jim played in the opening match against the United States in Hartford and then I was in goal for the second game against Colombia in Miami. It looked as if Craig was going to go down the road which Ron Greenwood had once gone down with England when he played Peter Shilton and Ray Clemence in alternate games for a spell. I didn't think that was a good idea back when the English tried it and I didn't think it was something which would work out well for Scotland either. I felt that Craig had to make up his mind and he also had to make it public in order to end the speculation. The longer it went on the more heated the arguments for and against myself and Jim got. We had spoken about it and we both felt that Craig should tell us early, giving the unlucky one time to handle the disappointment. It would also allow the one who *was* going to play to get himself focused on the games.

The worst thing for us was not knowing, and I still don't know why Craig kept it under wraps for so long. It was a hard shout for him, of course. It was obvious that both of us had strong claims to be the number one and so it was an extremely tough decision to make. Jim had never let the country down and I would argue that I hadn't done so either, even though the Finnish game kept being dragged back into the equation.

Finally, when we were down at Stratford at the hotel where we were to stay for the first series of games, Craig took us aside separately and told us what was happening. I was the one who got the call and I'm sure Jim went through the same agonies as I did in Italy when he was told he was not playing. This time, of course, Hodgy was looking after me at Ibrox as well as being with Scotland and, like me six years earlier, Jim must have felt that this would tip the scales ever so slightly in my favour. However, I know now that I was wrong to think that would be an issue. Alan Hodgkinson, when consulted by Craig Brown – as he is on all goalkeeping matters – will always make an honest decision. Personal feelings never come into it; being with Jim at Old Trafford and with me at Ibrox would not have entered his mind.

I had said to Craig as far back as the last qualifying game, when we knew that he had reached England and the finals, that he should tell the press of his decision. Yet he delayed it until just a few days before we were set to meet Holland at Villa Park in our first group game. Perhaps he wanted to avoid any kind of flak hitting the squad and disturbing the build-up, but I thought – and I'm certain that Jim was of the same mind – it was better out in the open.

At least once we knew we were able to talk about the games freely without wondering if we were saying the right things. I mean, I couldn't start talking about the Dutch forwards and how a goalkeeper should deal with Denis Bergkamp and then finish up sitting on the bench as a substitute with egg on my face. That wasn't on.

Still, Craig had to play it his way and it's difficult to question the Scotland team manager when you examine his record and have witnessed the attention to detail which marks everything that he does. It's easy for punters to have a go and give it the 'Craig who?' bit, just as they did when Andy Roxburgh was appointed to the job, and easier still for them to sit at home and say that Alex Ferguson or Kenny Dalglish or some other big-name manager should be appointed to take over Scotland. But to be fair, Craig has not had too many bad results. Nine times out of ten he has been able to put a team out on the field and get the result he has been seeking. OK, it doesn't always work, but you could say that about any team. Just when you think everything is going really well, along comes a game such as the one against Estonia in Monaco when we could only draw. Immediately we lost some of the advantage we had gained in our World Cup group.

That, though, was an exception. Most of the time Craig has been right on the button with his tactics and his team selections. Inevitably, he has taken stick when he has named the men he wants to play in certain games and he's been told that he has made mistakes before a ball has been kicked. But when you are manager of the national team you expect that, and I don't think it has ever been as bad in Scotland as it has down south or in some of the European countries where managers are hounded from their jobs when they get poor results. Still, it can be tough, and there are times when I feel that Craig hasn't been given enough credit. His biggest asset is his thoroughness. He can go through an opposition team man by man and tell you the individual strengths and weaknesses of every player. Then he can go on and tell you how they perform collectively. He is rarely wrong when it comes down to detail. Defenders are told how their opponents will react to certain on-field situations, forwards have their cards marked as to how their markers will attempt to stop them, and even the goalkeepers are briefed on how the strikers prefer to finish. Nothing is left to chance. Either Craig himself, his assistant manager Alex Miller, my old manager at Hibs, or some of the coaching staff from the SFA Headquarters at Park Gardens, watch the other countries as often as is humanly possible.

Perhaps I was trying to match that thoroughness when I decided that I did not want to play because I was still haunted by the calf muscle injury which had struck me down in Athens and again when I tried to return too soon against Partick Thistle in a game at Firhill.

Even now I can still remember the pain I felt each time it happened to me. In Athens I came out to clear a ball and felt something snap at the back of my leg. I just went down in agony and didn't know what had happened. At first I looked round to see if someone had thrown something at me because it was as if I had been struck by a missile – maybe even a pellet from an air gun. I was stretchered off.

A few weeks later it went again and yet everything had seemed OK. I had been receiving treatment and the specialist had taken a look at it. There had been a small tear in the calf muscle but X-rays had not suggested complications. The reason for the breakdown was a mystery.

Off I went to London again for further tests and more examinations and this time the specialist was able to find out what was wrong. He ordered an immediate operation because he discovered that a pocket of blood had gathered beneath the muscle, tucked away so that the earlier X-rays had not revealed it. Basically, the first time round no one was particularly looking for any kind of complication because it had appeared to be a simple enough calf tear.

What had happened was that the blood had gathered in a small balloon and it was this which had caused the new breakdown because I had placed pressure on the muscle. When this was removed, I was told, then the calf would simply be left to heal itself. It was something of a shock for me, though. Having expected a new training and treatment regime, I found myself being prepared for another operation. It wasn't something which filled me with confidence – as a footballer injuries always arouse a twinge of doubt, especially when they arrive so unexpectedly.

It also turned out to be more serious than I had originally thought. I was left with a lengthy scar after having 25 stitches and every time I looked at it I felt that something might go wrong again. That lived with me for quite a spell.

I wasn't able to play for the rest of that season so when the Scotland game arrived so quickly I was still unprepared. If the same set of circumstances loomed in front of me in the future I would do the same again. It was not club before country, nor would it be that in the future. It was never as simple as that. I agonised over that decision and I still say it was the right one for the team as well as the right one for me. Only people who have suffered injury could fully understand.

I was certainly prepared for the fact that Craig Brown might just jettison me. After all, he had done that with one Rangers player already. When Andy Roxburgh had been Scotland manager, Richard Gough criticised him and found himself banished from the squad. When Craig stepped into the job, Goughie made it plain that he held no grudges and would be happy to play for his country again. There was quite a bandwagon in favour of his return, but Craig resisted and showed a strength of purpose which most Scotland fans might not have expected to see from him. So I was aware of what I was going in against. If Craig had thought I was just pulling out for club reasons then he would never have considered me again. I would have been a non-person as far as Scotland was concerned, in the same way as my club captain was. But Craig, possibly because his own career had been interrupted by injuries, recognised the dilemma which faced me. He understood that I would be going into the game – if I was selected – with the thought of injury on my mind, and that wasn't going to help anyone.

He stood by me when it was difficult for him to do so and I have never forgotten that. His commitment to his players is paramount, and the lads appreciate that. There has been a great deal of talk about the team spirit which exists among the players, and most of that is down to Craig and his backroom staff. They encourage the feel of a club team and they try very, very hard to show loyalty as often and as long as they can. That has worked for them. The current Scotland squad doesn't have as many big names as previous squads have had – although I do believe that some of the players don't get enough credit for their skills – yet the success rate has been high and the organisation and fitness of the teams have been exceptional. Sure, the players get along, but the added chemistry which is required comes from Craig Brown's leadership and the input of the people he has surrounded himself with behind the scenes.

They have not simply created a club feeling; they have been able to put in place a powerful bond which has helped the team in bad times and lifted them to some special performances. Craig will not tamper with the formula he has found successful, and nor should he. His record speaks for him. Anyone looking through the statistics has to be aware of what he has achieved and even the Tartan Army have learned to appreciate that it's not always necessary to have a glamorous, big-name manager to make a success of a national team. Detail, determination and diligence do bring their rewards.

4 Dressing-Room Punch-Ups

WITH ALL THE HYPE surrounding our nine-in-a-row title bid and Celtic trying to save their long-standing record, last season found us besieged by rumour after rumour.

It's never easy to avoid rumours at Ibrox. We've had more than our share of bad publicity over the years and I haven't done a great deal to help the club or myself on occasions. Perhaps it has something to do with the fact that there are no major film or television personalities in Scotland. Down south the tabloid newspapers tend to focus on the soap opera personalities, the top models or the pop stars, while in Glasgow they home in on footballers.

Last year was particularly bad and in the brief moments they were leaving Paul Gascoigne in peace I came in for my share of the stick. Believe me, there are times when you feel that you're being stalked and Gazza has suffered more than most. He is almost unable to leave the house without being followed, and it's an awful feeling knowing that people are watching your every move. Of course, there's not a whole lot we can do about it unless we decide to live the very quietest of lives – and that's asking a little too much. We all train hard – and when you do that you also want to play hard. Most footballers enjoy a drink once a game is over and your job has been done. Yet you can't always do that because you have the public hassling you and people trying to set you up in some kind of way so that a picture can be taken.

On a number of occasions someone has called up a newspaper and told them that we were in trouble in a bar and then, after arranging to pick up a few quid, the guy has then gone about *starting* the trouble. That's the kind of thing that goes on. I can't pretend it doesn't make me really angry. If you're a footballer in London you can enjoy a night out without being hounded but in Glasgow I can't do that. And in Edinburgh, where I still live, it's even worse. In Glasgow I only have to worry about Celtic fans giving me trouble because I know that our own mob won't bother me, but in Edinburgh the Hearts fans hate me because I once played for Hibs and the Hibs fans hate me even more because I left Easter Road and joined up at Ibrox. There is no hiding place for me and there are only a couple of places where I can have a drink without being bothered.

The fans I dislike the most are not the Celtic fans, as you'd probably expect, but the crowd which follow Hibs. I played at Easter Road for four years and I made a lot of important saves for them and did my bit to help them into Europe. As soon as I left to go to Rangers in the summer of 1991, however, I was pilloried. That hurt me deeply; much more than anything else in football has ever hurt me.

When I went out to play for Rangers against Hibs for the first time after my transfer, the jeering and the abuse I received was incredible. It didn't help me any that I lost a goal that night. And to make matters worse, it was the semi-final of the Skol Cup and the one goal from Keith Wright sent us out of the tournament. Hibs, of course, went on to win. That just had to be in the script, didn't it? I left Hibs because I wanted to win medals and the first trophy of the new season finished up at Easter Road!

Seriously, though, the bitterness has never diminished and I honestly believe that the Hibs supporters are the worst football supporters in the country – and I say that mindful of the troubles we have had at Aberdeen in recent seasons. I was even assaulted on the field when we played in Edinburgh a couple of seasons back. I haven't been the sole target for their venom either. As far as I'm concerned the former club manager, Alex Miller, who is now assistant to Gordon Strachan at Coventry, was driven out by fan power. They never accepted him, no matter how well he did.

Managing Hibs is a difficult, difficult job, yet Alex did it for a long time and gave the club a degree of success which others might not have been able to provide. He also made them a profit on transfer deals, selling players for big bucks, and then operated on not much more than a shoestring budget when it came to bringing in players to replace those he had been forced to sell. None of that was ever taken into account by a hardcore of fans. All that mattered was that Alex Miller had spent seventeen years as a player with Rangers, which to them was the kiss of death. His ability did not count one little bit, and they chose to ignore the fact that he had spent time as a manager at Morton and St Mirren after finishing his playing career.

It's their loss. Alex Miller has no need to prove his professionalism – it has been acknowledged by Coventry and also by Scotland, where he has been Craig Brown's trusted lieutenant ever since the Scotland manager moved into the job.

But it's that kind of behaviour which makes it so hard for us all. And when the rumours kick in, things often become even worse.

Last season, as well as the usual nonsense about pub and club brawls and restaurant bans and general misbehaviour, it spread across the country that I had punched Brian Laudrup after a game at Easter Road when he had missed a crucial penalty. (In fact, he actually missed the kick twice after being given the chance to retake it.) We lost the game, missed out on three valuable points and allowed Celtic an opportunity to cut into our lead. According to the press, I was so enraged by this that I whacked the best player I have ever played alongside!

When it reached my ears I obviously denied it, as did my mates when they heard the story. Brian denied it. All the lads rubbished it . . . but it persisted. For weeks the stories grew until they reached the level that Brian had told manager Walter Smith that he would never again play in the same team as me. This was gospel. There were no doubts surrounding this story. It was now a case of Walter Smith putting me up for sale again to ensure that Brian remained at Ibrox. Goram simply had to be sacrificed. On and on the rumours rolled. One story even had me taking a wild swing at Brian, missing him and knocking out the club secretary Campbell Ogilvie. I had newspapermen calling me and saying that the story was going to run that the club were throwing me out because of the dressing-room punch-up.

All of it was nonsense. Brian Laudrup is the last guy on earth I would take a poke at. Last summer, when we were playing pre-season warm-up games in Denmark, my wife Tracy and our son Lewis stayed at Brian's home with his wife and family, on the Danish coast not far from Copenhagen. I certainly wasn't going to repay him for his kindness with a punch. Brian is an absolute gentleman, without a bad bone in his body, and you just couldn't fall out with him. Admittedly, it had not been one of the best afternoons of my life, given the stick I have to take at Easter Road, but you simply suffer it. OK, Brian might have made a mistake but all of us make mistakes at times during the season and I'm certainly not immune.

What happened that day was over and done with. It hurt at the time but all I said to Brian, who was sitting at the other side of the dressing room with his head down, was: 'Why did you take the second penalty?' It didn't go beyond that because Brian didn't need anyone to tell him that he had missed the penalty at the second time of asking. He knew that only too well.

Brian had scored from the penalty spot before and so he was the one who stepped up to take it. He missed, but one of the Hibs players had moved into the penalty box as he struck the ball and so it was retaken. Somehow Brian missed it again – and that was us beaten for the first time in the Premier League that season and against a team we had hammered 4-0 in the Coca-Cola Cup a month earlier. But it was just a very unfortunate mistake, and anyone can suffer that way. Brian's made a massive contribution to the club since joining up at Ibrox and is honestly the best player I have ever played with. Sorry Gazza, you're just a little bit behind. Maybe two inches behind . . .

Eventually the 'fight' became a joke between us, and whenever Brian misses a chance in a game – and that's not too often – I'll say to him, 'Maybe I should have belted you at Easter Road.' At least we can laugh about it now, even though it should never have happened in the first place.

Sometimes you *do* get incidents inside the dressing room when players fall out. It has certainly happened at our place because we have a bunch of very strong characters and you can always expect to get a bit of stick when you do something wrong. You learn to accept it too – unless you feel it is undeserved. Then you have to stand your corner and defend your position and that's what did get me into trouble in my second season. It happened during a match with Aberdeen at Ibrox in August 1992. The former Celtic player, Roy Aitken, now the manager at Pittodrie, was playing for the club then and he scored with a long-range shot in the first half. Like most people, I don't like being made to look foolish – which I did as his shot went flying past me. Even more annoying was the fact that it was a one-time Celtic player who got the goal. I thought that he should have been and could have been closed down a bit earlier as he broke forward. It seemed to me that we had allowed him too much room and that was where the mistake was really made. I said so too.

I shouted to Nigel Spackman that he should have been in to make a challenge much more quickly than he did. Needless to say, he didn't agree, but his attitude suggested to me that he knew it was his mistake but was going to cover up rather than own up. I didn't like that at all and when we went into the dressing room at half-time I was still seething. I started on him again and he threw some abuse back at me, calling me a 'fat bastard'. I cracked. I jumped over the treatment table and let him have it. After belting him twice, he went down and curled up on the floor like a hedgehog as I was dragged away. I'd lost it totally.

I was shoved into the little area in the dressing room which the physio uses until I'd cooled down. Thankfully it all happened before the gaffer arrived.

In the second half we went on to win the game and the incident was more or less forgotten, as these flare-ups usually are.

Looking back, I suppose I was bang out of order, and even if I had been determined to take up the issue with him, I should at least have waited until the end of the game. There was no lasting feud between us, however, because coincidentally Nigel was sold by the club within weeks of the barney. I was more worried about what the manager might do because I knew that while he had missed the blows being struck he was aware that something had happened and that I had been involved. I expected to be summoned up the 'marbles' to be given a warning but he surprised me. Instead of the formal bit he just came up alongside me in training, just as we were jogging around the track, and said quietly, 'I know what you did. And I don't want any repeat of it in the future. OK?' That was it but I knew he would not tolerate another similar incident. This half-time cabaret wasn't quite what he was after.

However, I think he recognised that these things do happen and in the heat of the moment any little slight can boil over into something far more serious. Basically, in a team game such as football, there are always going to be little bust-ups because players want to win games. When mistakes are made then blame naturally follows and sometimes it seems as if we are being asked to carry too much responsibility. That's when defensiveness comes into play and rows start. It's all part of the territory, especially when you're with a big club such as Rangers.

I do regret the fact that I didn't get the opportunity to apologise properly to Nigel before he left the club. I wasn't sorry for my reaction because these things do happen at all clubs in the heat of the moment, but Nigel Spackman did a tremendous job for the club in the two or three seasons he was at Ibrox and he didn't deserve me flying off the handle at him.

Someone could have taken a swing at me last season when I lost a terrible goal against Aberdeen at Pittodrie, yet the lads didn't say anything. Nor did the gaffer. I think they recognised how bad I felt. I didn't say anything to them either because there was nothing I could say which could lift the gloom. I had cost the club two points that afternoon and it wasn't easy to accept that.

It was a goal which should never have been: a goal which was totally my fault. People did ask me afterwards if the ball had moved in the wind but I'm not going to hide behind any excuses. Somehow I lost concentration at a vital moment – don't ask me how it happened – and as the ball came towards me I misjudged the flight and made a total mess of attempting to stop it. It was a nightmare moment for me. I saw the ball heading for the goal line and I just couldn't recover in time to stop it going over. I really wished the ground would simply open up as the Aberdeen fans jeered at me from behind the goal.

I was the last to get changed in the dressing room after the game. A few of the lads did try to console me without speaking. Lauders, Coisty and Alan McLaren all patted me on the head because they knew I was taking it badly.

To make matters worse, so much was made of the mistake in the press, but eventually I consoled myself with the thought that so many headlines about a single error must mean I don't make all that many. Even the gaffer told the press after the game that it demonstrated I was 'human'.

I'm not being boastful but I have had a good record over the years I have been with Rangers. I have made mistakes – all goalkeepers make mistakes – but real bloomers such as that one at Aberdeen have not been part of my game. Having said that, I realised then that the goal could have had an effect on the title race and I had to live with that for a week or two. Not the most pleasant of times for me!

The day after the game I just wanted to put the whole thing behind me but with the full glare of publicity surrounding the incident, it wasn't really possible. I knew I would have to ride out the storm – but I hoped I could take a break from training on the Monday and let the worry that I might do the same again get out of my system. I felt I should get away from playing until my confidence was fully restored.

The gaffer had other ideas. On the Monday and Tuesday he had me involved in training games and, looking back, I believe he was right.

By the time the first training game was over I felt better. It was enough to tell me that I hadn't lost my confidence and the other players were really understanding. They must have sensed how bad I felt, because normally you're slaughtered in the dressing room after a blunder of that kind. This time, though, there was no stick flying around. The main men who would have been involved in that, Coisty and Durranty, actually helped me through it. They were good as gold about it. Mind you, I know there will be a day of reckoning. Just when I think it's forgotten, that's when they'll start.

That, though, is the kind of dressing room we have and it is the strength of feeling among the players which has helped us to win so many trophies and place so many records into the history books. Sure, they will hand out some abuse when it's deserved, but they will also be there to help you through the really hard times. There is a camaraderie which has brought us real consistency over the years. The lads will point out your mistakes but they will also all be there to pick you up and get you going again. It's been one of the best dressing rooms I have operated in. There's no doubt that when things are right in there, when all the lads can pull together and work and train and play together, you will get success.

Sometimes it's hard to live up to the unwritten code at Ibrox. There are occasions when you feel like lashing out if someone's criticising you, but that would be the wrong thing to do because the lads are trying to help. The criticism can be harsh but it is always meant to be constructive.

Knowing that the other players are judging you helps ensure that you don't drop your standards on the field. Your pride as a professional is at stake and that is what counts most at Ibrox. We all get criticised at one time or another and the fact that the manager encourages a strong dressing room has been an important factor for Rangers. And yes, we let our hair down on occasion, which we are criticised for, but tell me anyone who doesn't enjoy a few drinks with their mates when work is over?

There is a code of discipline at the club – and Walter Smith hammers us whenever we step out of line – but I think he realises that because we are under so much pressure and constantly living in the full glare of publicity, there are times when we have to relax. We have times when we all go out for a drink together and that's something which has prevented any cliques springing up at the club. Despite the differences we might have on occasion after games – or even during games – we genuinely get on well together as a group.

Our occasional excursions have inevitably attracted

some adverse publicity, but the tabloids have always had some kind of fascination for Rangers and their players. It's obviously not the type of attention that any of us enjoy – and poor Gazza has often been a virtual prisoner in his home in Renfrewshire when the media simply won't leave him alone – but we have to live with it.

My genuine hope is that the public at large and especially the Rangers supporters recognise that we are not as bad as we are sometimes portrayed and that it would be more sensible if we were judged on our achievements on the field. This squad of players has racked up record after record and these will all be in the history books long after the various stories about boozing and the rest have been forgotten.

I think it's fair to say that most of the players who have come to Ibrox have been real professionals – we wouldn't have been able to win the trophies we have if we weren't. It's also true that most of us joined Rangers because we wanted to win medals – and that's what we have been able to do. Every professional footballer wants to have something tangible to show for his years in the game. Take my own situation. After ten years with Oldham and Hibs I didn't have a single medal. I was fortunate enough to have a few Scotland international caps but there was nothing from my time as a pro with my two senior clubs to indicate that I had done anything out of the ordinary.

Rangers changed all that, but it would not have happened if we hadn't all shown a professionalism when going about our jobs. The former Rangers manager Graeme Souness used to tell stories about Liverpool. The great team he was such an important part of were not averse to going out on a few bevvy sessions either, but when it came to winning games both in England and in Europe, very few could match them. If we were as undisciplined as the often lurid headlines make us out to be, we would never have achieved the consistency we have shown over a long period of time. It would have been impossible.

A study in concentration.
A goalkeeper can never afford to lose track of the game for even a second.

Above The two goalkeepers who were once such rivals for the Scotland position remain the best of friends off the pitch – Andy Goram with Jim Leighton.

Below Andy Goram pulls off a penalty save from Hibs' striker and Scotland team mate Darren Jackson during a Premier League match.

bove Ally McCoist has become one of Andy Goram's closest friends. His advice and
encouragement were vital to Goram when Rangers' Manager Walter Smith placed Andy on
the transfer list.

elow Andy Goram and Rangers' Manager Walter Smith receive their Player and Manager of
the Year awards in May 1993. A year later, Smith was ready to sell his star keeper after
Goram's booze-up in Tenerife.

Danish player Brian Laudrup and Frenchman Basile Boli arrived at Ibrox at the same time in 1994. Laudrup went on to become a major star with the club but Boli left, according to Andy Goram because he did not want to mix with the other Rangers players.

chard Gough, the former Rangers Captain was an 'inspirational figure' according to Goram ho played behind him throughout Rangers' Glory run. Gough left Rangers at the end of the 1996/97 season to pursue a new career in America with Kansas City Wiz.

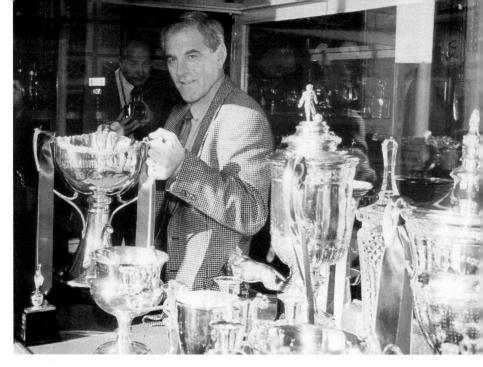

Above Rangers Manager Walter Smith with some of the silverware which has become a permanent fixture in the Ibrox trophy room.

Below The English contingent at Ibrox. Nigel Spackman (*second left*) got on well with his countrymen Chris Woods, Terry Butcher and Mark Walters. He did not enjoy the same sort of camaraderie with Goram who punched him in a dressing room brawl at half time during the game against Aberdeen at Ibrox in August 1992.

ht The Great Dane, Brian
*Laud*rup – '... the best player I've
*eve*r played with', says Goram,
and one of the nicest men in the
*ga*me'.

*Bel*ow Monaco midfielder John
*Col*lins was a team mate of
*Go*ram's at Hibs and then a rival
*wh*en he played for Celtic. Goram
*bel*ieves he is one of the most
*de*dicated professionals he has
*ev*er encountered.

John Brown, now a coach at Ibrox, was part of Goram's favourite defensive line-up and is se
here winning a challenge against Marseilles' German international striker Rudi Voeller durin
Rangers' epic European Champions League run during the 1992/93 season.

We work hard at Rangers and anyone who thinks otherwise should come to the pre-season training at Ciocco in the Tuscany hills. That's as tough a regime as you would get at any club anywhere and the expectations of the training staff could not be more demanding. That is where the fitness levels for the season are determined and if you vary in weight for no good reason during the season then you're in trouble.

There are times when the sheer professionalism which is always there at Ibrox is seriously underestimated. We play hard but we work hard, first of all, and I don't see anything wrong with that. I know that people will disagree with me, and perhaps I don't look the perfect athlete, but I do my job as everyone at Ibrox does and if there are any arguments about how we go about that then the answers are there in the game's history books. No other Rangers team can match what we have achieved and it is on that we should be judged and, indeed, will be judged in future years. I'm sure of that.

5 Dead Men's Tendons

NJURIES HAVE DOGGED ME in my time with Rangers, the worst being my damaged cruciate ligament which saw me making the 6,000-mile journey to Los Angeles and the hospital in Sherman Oaks which specialises in the treatment of that particular type of injury. Eight Rangers players have been there now to undergo surgery – which consists of taking a dead man's tendon and replacing your ligament with that. Obviously it is highly specialised, which is why we have to travel so far.

Like so many of the other injuries which crop up in the game today, ligament damage is becoming more and more prevalent. There is little doubt that the number of games the top players are asked to take part in contributes to this injury toll. Four of the Scottish players from Euro 96 have had surgery and I think it's something like as many as fourteen of the English players have been out of action at some time or another since then too. We're not talking about injuries players used to suffer from either; these are stress injuries caused by playing too many matches. Just look at the schedule I had during the build-up to the European Championship in England and you will see the demands made on many of the leading players in recent years. Rangers finished the season, remember, by taking part in the Scottish Cup Final.

By then I had been involved in more than 50 games and two days after winning the Cup I was off to America where we had warm-up games against the United States and Colombia. Once there we found ourselves being trained hard because Craig Brown and Alex Miller felt that, even considering the long season, we had to be especially fit to withstand the rigours of a major tournament in England. So this was no take-it-easy holiday jaunt. After the ten days there, we were allowed a few days' break with our families and then we were off to England for more training and eventually the three group games against Holland, England and Switzerland.

Of course, we didn't qualify for the next phase of the competition and by mid-June we were back home, knowing that because of the early date given to the European Cup preliminary round we would have to be back training at the club early in July. Pre-season work and then games in Denmark followed, to prepare for the match we had to face against the Russian champions from Vladikavkaz. We were back on the treadmill . . .

I'm not trying to suggest that it is only Rangers who suffer this sort of programme. It is fast becoming the norm for *all* clubs who are successful at home and then find themselves taking part in the European tournaments. This is the kind of schedule which is being forced on players all over Europe and there appears to be no way of escaping it any more. There seem to be more and more games every season. Something has to give and, sadly, it's the fitness of the players which is giving way first.

It annoys me when I see Rangers being criticised for the training methods which are employed by the club. Suggestions that we pick up so many injuries because we don't train properly are nonsense. The number of injuries at our club is connected quite clearly with the number of matches we have to play – and the number of matches which are crucially important. We find ourselves playing football almost the whole year round and that can't be right. Unfortunately, the only changes we've seen so far are that there are now two ties in the preliminary rounds of Europe, the pre-qualification for the Champions' League, and the first one or two matches have to be played in July before our domestic season has even begun! How can that make any sense? But Europe has decreed that this is what happens and we must follow their rules. It isn't going to do anything for our general fitness.

You also find the international team with matches which can only be played in the close season. These are usually important qualifying matches, so there have to be training games too in order for adequate preparations to be made. And so it goes on. If you qualify for the finals of the major international tournaments, you are looking at just two years between the World Cup and the European Championship. So a successful team is in action during the summer months when players should ideally be resting.

I am convinced that it was that kind of schedule which brought about my first major injury. There was one specific incident which sparked off the trouble but the fact that there was no time for rest and recovery guaranteed that I would require an operation. A break from the punishing schedule that season might have saved me the worries that surgery brings but it just wasn't possible. The incident occurred in an away game against Bruges, the Belgian champions, at the start of March 1993. This was the season when Rangers won the treble at home and were desperately close to reaching the European Cup Final. When the injury hit me we still had two more Champions' League games left to play; two matches which could carry us into the final ahead of Marseille. We had to face Bruges again at Ibrox and then the Russian champions, CSKA Moscow, also at home. The last thing I wanted was to miss out on the run up to the title and the important Scottish Cup games. It happened so simply, too.

There was a ball played through the middle and I came out of goal to cut it off and clear. Big Dave McPherson, who was playing at right back for us, was shepherding it back carefully. Behind him was Bruges striker Daniel Amokachi, the Nigerian international who later signed for Everton, and he was trying to get a foot to the ball as Dave tried to prevent him making contact. It was one of those awkward situations, and it was fairly obvious that Amokachi was going to slide in eventually. Which he did, but the way he went for the ball made it necessary for Dave to slide in as well. As he did so his boot caught me right on the leg, just under the knee. At the time, I didn't realise how serious the damage was, but the way the leg was jerked back meant that the posterior cruciate ligament was torn. The club doctor knew this – he's an expert on this kind of injury – and he warned me that I would need an operation at the end of the season if not before.

Before was out of the question because of the run of games we had, so I just nursed it a bit, missing a game or two here and there, but made it to the Cup Final and the win we had there against Aberdeen. A few days later I was off to the States for the operation. It was suggested that I should be over there three or four days before the operation was to be performed, probably to allow the knee to recover from the long flight and my body to adjust to the eight hours' time difference. The doc travelled with me to make sure everything was OK and Tracy was set to join me the day after the operation.

I have to be honest. I'm not the bravest of people when it comes to surgery. Durranty had been through the same thing and was very positive, assuring me that I would be playing again in no time at all, that there would be no ill-effects and that the operation itself was a breeze. But I wasn't wholly convinced, despite the fact that my injury was not as bad as his had been. The specialist who examined him said later that the only time he had ever seen a knee as badly damaged was when the patient had been in a car crash.

Obviously you worry about the future and whether you

will play again – and I do tend to think the worst. When I went into the clinic the night before the operation I couldn't sleep, even after taking sleeping pills. When they took me down to surgery for the operation the next morning, I was still conscious. Seeing all the surgeon's equipment lying around – the saws and the mallets and the needles and the scalpels – did nothing for my nerves.

The next thing I knew I was in bed, back in my room, but with drips and tubes all around and a terrible gnawing pain around my knee. Typically, I jumped to the wrong conclusion straight away. The operation had obviously gone wrong.

In panic, I rang for the nurses, who very calmly explained that the tubes were there to drain away fluid from the knee and gave me morphine for the pain. I felt better after that – not least because they had explained to me what was happening – but over the next few hours it seemed as if I was ringing the little emergency button almost constantly in a bid to take the pain away. Durranty hadn't mentioned this!

The next day the physio arrived, got me out of bed, gave me a walking frame and told me to walk up and down the ward. It was agony and I told her so in no uncertain terms. But she didn't seem to hear me, and made me carry on. Even with tears of pain running down my face, she wouldn't let me stop. Naturally I told the doc what had happened when he came to visit later, and thankfully he spoke to the staff and told them they had to allow me time to recover. It seemed they wanted the rehabilitation process to start straight away, probably not realising that the club would have a special programme laid out for me when I returned to Glasgow.

When I was released we spent a few days in Santa Monica, and then Tracy, the doc and I went to Phoenix in Arizona for a rest. Arranged by the club, we stayed in one of the best hotels I have ever been in. It says a great deal for the chairman that he looks after players in this way. It's not just the operation which is important; it is also the recovery. The chairman knows this, so you get the finest medical treatment and first-class recuperation surroundings. I honestly believe that if I had been at a smaller club my career might have been over by now. At Rangers they see the players as the club's major asset and nothing is too good for you. They don't mollycoddle you though; I genuinely needed rest and there was no way I could take a long flight home so soon after surgery.

I had a brace on my left knee and could only walk by using crutches. The metal brace was there to prevent me from moving it at all; it is crucial that you don't bend the knee after the operation because that would affect the work which had been done in the operating theatre. The new ligament has to have time to settle in – though it isn't actually a ligament they use at all in this process. Instead they use an Achilles' tendon, which is the strongest tendon in your body and therefore gives extra strength to the knee.

I must admit, the thought that I had somebody else's Achilles' tendon in me was rather strange. Apparently, the tendon is split into three pieces and then plaited together – just as you would plait hair – in order to replace a damaged ligament. Gruesome, isn't it?

There is always the possibility that your body will reject the tendon – just as there is in all 'spare parts' surgery – but mine was OK. The problem, however, lay in the fact that I couldn't do anything for myself. Tracy was basically my nurse during that recuperation period, having to change my dressings daily, help me dress and even assist me when I was hobbling around the hotel pool. We were in Arizona for ten days and the heat was soaring above the 100 degree mark – how I wished I could jump into that pool. But it was a matter of staying in the shade and hoping that the enforced rest would help the knee mend enough to allow the stitches to be removed on schedule. All went to plan, apart from the size of the needle the doctor pulled out to drain the fluid with when I returned to the clinic. I almost fainted when I saw it!

He assured me that in six months' time I would be OK and playing again, echoing what everyone had already said. But I still had worries over the future. There had been a whole lot of self-examination in Arizona. I began to think I would never be able to play again; that I was doomed when I had only just begun at Ibrox. There were a few tears shed in that Arizona hotel because I had felt that I was approaching the very best years of my career. We had just completed a superb season – one of the finest seasons in the long, distinguished history of the club – and it had been the best of times for all of us involved. Now it seemed that it was all going to be snatched away from me – and from Tracy. Suddenly the future didn't look as bright as it had done a few short weeks earlier, when we were parading the Scottish Cup in front of our supporters. Now all I had was this feeling of foreboding; a nagging doubt that no matter what the specialists told me or what Durranty had said to me before I left, the recovery might not go as everyone expected. Part of the reason for my feelings at this time, of course, was the pain. I hadn't been told about that. No one had said just how bad that would be and so it hit me severely because it never, ever seemed to ease off. It was there constantly. Throbbing. Gnawing. Never allowing me to forget what I had been through and what lay ahead. Flying back was a problem because of the way the leg had to be placed, so I went first class – another demonstration of how Rangers treat their players – because there was more room for me to keep the leg straight and avoid bending the knee. Even then I needed painkillers to get me through the flight.

Pre-season, the gaffer invited me to Il Ciocco along with the first-team squad, just to keep me involved, I suppose, but I still wasn't allowed to do anything. The brace had to remain in place for two months or more, so all I could do was limp down to the training ground and watch the lads work and Alan Hodgkinson do the specialist training with Ally Maxwell. Maxie had been bought by the club when I was injured.

They needed experienced cover and he was going to be the number one goalkeeper at the club when the season started. My own comeback was not scheduled until around the New Year, but at that time I couldn't even begin to think of a return. I used to end up standing in goal while Hodgy hit the balls to me, which I caught without moving the knee at all. Desperate to do anything, I was happy to be doing even that. Then I'd walk away and maybe kick a ball back into play for the lads and the doc would be after me, telling me not to do anything like that because I couldn't afford to take the slightest risk. It's ironic that throughout my footballing life I've hated pre-season training – all that running and hard work – and yet right then I would have given anything to be allowed to get involved. Patience is not one of my virtues, but I knew that if I attempted to do too much too soon it might mean another seven or eight months on the side-lines and another operation. There was no way I wanted to contemplate that.

At the same time as I had the cruciate operation, the surgeon had done some tidying up around both knees, performing what are called lateral releases. Over the years the wear and tear I had suffered had taken both knees out of alignment; your knees are set in a kind of groove but mine had moved, so that the knee caps were rubbing against other bones. Having this corrected meant that my return date was delayed a little longer. Initially I had been told to think in terms of six months out but that stretched on to almost nine. More and more I found myself thinking about the future, which was unusual for me because I had never been one to plan ahead. As a footballer, all you think about is the next game, and the one after that, and when that's suddenly taken away from you, your mind turns to other matters. It was fairly traumatic having to think about what I might do if I was forced to give up the game. A friend of mine offered us a pub to run and that was one option. Mind you, a pub was all I needed . . .

It's that feeling that you're going to have to start again, doing something new, that wears you down. And so you drink too much and get depressed. It's only when you speak to other players who have faced up to the same thing that you discover that it's common. I remember Mark Hateley telling me how he went through agonies when he suffered a bad injury abroad. He used to just sit and get drunk and that's not like the big man at all. The fear that everything is going to be taken away from you is all-consuming. For most of us football is all we've known. You start off as a kid with a club and you go straight on through the system to become a full pro, without experiencing any other way of life. You're protected from the rest of the world to a large extent because everything is done for you at the club – and the bigger the club then the more there is done for you. To have to imagine a future without all of that – one where you are going to be sent out there to fend for yourself – is not a scenario any footballer relishes.

When you see some of the lads who have stopped playing – many because of injuries – you know how much they miss the game and everything that comes with it. Scott Nisbet comes back to Ibrox quite a lot, and you can sense that he would just love to be back playing, back as one of the lads. There's a glint in their eyes whenever they step through the dressing-room door. That kind of thing makes you realise just how valuable the game is to you.

It's not easy getting back to the level of fitness required to start playing again, and I spent a long time down at Lilleshall at the Football Association rehab. centre. We were sending so many players down there that the gaffer eventually hired their physio, Grant Downie, to come up and work at Ibrox! I can't pretend I enjoyed myself at Lilleshall but what kept me going was Durranty. He had to spend 51 weeks there building up his knee after his operation. What an inspiration. All of us who have followed down the same road – to Los Angeles, Lilleshall and back into the game – have seen him as an example. The character and the sheer courage Durranty demonstrated was incredible.

Of course, I have had other injuries since then. Most of them, like the calf muscle problem I've already mentioned, have occurred in the other leg because I was instinctively trying to protect my damaged knee. None of them have been career-threatening, though, and after all my worrying, the operation was a success. While I can't train with the other players like I used to do, I am able to do all the specialist work which Hodgy plans for me. The short, sharp work is OK and the goalkeeper training is fine, but if I was asked to do a half-hour run I couldn't do it. Unsurprisingly, the lads give me a bit of stick about that, claiming that I never do any training at all, but they know Hodgy demands a lot from me in our two days together. He doesn't let up at all, and it's down to him that I came back from the ligament operation so successfully. He was always there to encourage me, mapping out the type of programme which kept me fit while protecting my knee. It hasn't been easy for him either.

In fact, so successful has my recovery been that I am still able to play 50 or more games in a season and I can still hold down my first-team place with Rangers and Scotland. All of that after the months of dark despair when I felt I would never play again. Now all I have to worry about is when I might have to stop playing because my career has simply come to an end, and that will be really hard. Players have told me that you know yourself when the time comes but it doesn't make it any easier. However, if I start making a fool of myself out there on the pitch and end up letting the other players down because my timing or confidence has gone, that's when I'll walk away from the game.

The problem is where to go. It's a question every player has to consider: not everyone can be a manager or a coach and not everyone wants to take that route anyway. A lot of ex-players seem to drift into another life, and I expect that's what will happen to me. I don't even like to think about it. I'm 33 years old now, but that's not too bad for a goalie when you consider that Jim Leighton is six years older and is starting all over again with Aberdeen.

What I do know is that I've been lucky enough to have had a long career and I can only hope there are more good times to come. I do wonder about the younger lads coming into the game, though. The demands are ridiculous and you find that players who are only just starting out on their careers are already carrying injuries which would normally only affect them in their later years, if at all. Take Rangers player Charlie Miller, who is only in his early twenties but was suffering from shin splints last season. Stephen Wright, who is not much older, has been on the Los Angeles journey like myself, as has the new signing from Chile, Sebastian Rozental. Across the city at Celtic Park, Phil O'Donnell has had constant injury problems as has young Brian O'Neil. The people who run the game should be looking at ways and means of cutting down the number of games. If they don't then new players will find that their careers have ended before they've even started. I'm extremely fortunate that everything worked out OK for me when it came to that major operation, but when you look at the groin and pelvic injuries littering the game today you have to recognise the toll that the huge number of matches is taking on the modern player. I have been through the agonies which accompany a serious injury and had to grapple with the idea that my career could be ending. I have had to go through the tortures of rehabilitation at Lilleshall and then fight to get my place back in the team. I'm not alone in that, of course, but I do think it gives me the right to spell out where things are going wrong in the game today. There is no question that the major cause of injuries now is stress, nor is there any doubt that some of the ligament injuries which afflict so many players are worse than a fracture. It used to be that a leg break was the worst thing that could happen to any player but that's no longer the case. A player can recover from a break with little difficulty but serious ligament damage can keep you out of action for a very long time and there is always the chance that it will recur. Persistent groin problems are similar; they often bring long-term damage which is far more serious than most fractures. Yet still the authorities talk about more and more games, and when they do so they are talking in the main about big games, because that's what television wants, not to mention the sponsors and the supporters.

Players will get less and less recovery time between the major matches, and that will lead to occasions when they will be asked to take painkillers by their clubs – or even volunteer to take them because they don't want to miss out on a vital game. That can cause still more problems, either by helping to end a career prematurely or bringing injuries which will persist when your playing days are over.

I took a jag to play in the Scottish Cup tie against Celtic last season and I did the same thing against Dundee United in a Premier League game (strangely we lost them both!), but in those particular cases I had been suffering from a rib injury which was painful but not the kind of thing which was going to be aggravated during the games. I wasn't putting myself at risk in any way and I know that the club would not favour anyone doing that if the possibility of long-term damage was there. But players may opt for it in situations where playing in a certain game is very important. There are always games that you really, desperately want to take part in. I have missed almost two seasons during my Rangers career and that has been a major disappointment for me. I don't want to miss too many more because there is always a certain thought lurking at the back of your mind. As Richard Gough has said so often: 'Enjoy it now because you just never know when your last game will be.'

6 Hodgy and the Goalkeeping Mafia

THINK IT'S REASONABLE to say that only goalkeepers can
understand other goalkeepers. Few people understand
me as well as Alan Hodgkinson does, my coach of
many years both at club and international level. This
is the man who first made me *think* about keeping goal.
Before he arrived in my life I was just stumbling through
my career, trying my best to learn from the mistakes I
made – and there were always a few of those – and relying
mainly on my instincts, my reflexes and my timing. I had
a fair amount of natural ability, which is what had taken
me into the game in the first place, and in my young days
I genuinely felt that that was all I needed. It was Hodgy
who taught me differently and turned round my entire
career, although I did not rate him one little bit when he
first arrived at Oldham to put me through my paces.
Quite honestly, I didn't know what he was talking about
to begin with, nor did I understand what he was attempting to do through his specialised training, possibly
because I thought I could amble along and teach myself
rather than bother with the technical side of keeping goal.

I did have a point. I had already won a couple of
Scotland international caps while I was still with Oldham
in the (old) English Second Division. Alex Ferguson, who
was with Aberdeen at the time and caretaker manager of
Scotland after the death of Jock Stein, gave me my first
honour when he sent me on as a substitute for Jim

Leighton in a warm-up game for the 1986 World Cup finals against East Germany at Hampden. Then he picked me for another Hampden game against Romania and a match away from home against Holland. I didn't lose a goal in any of them, which obviously helped me into the squad for the finals in Mexico. So you can see why I believed my natural abilities were enough to carry me through; making it to the World Cup finals and heading for Mexico from Boundary Park in Oldham was something of a quantum leap. There I was, with players such as Graeme Souness, Charlie Nicholas, Gordon Strachan and Steve Archibald, and I really thought I was on the way up. Over in Mexico – and also in the States before we went to the finals – I trained with Jim Leighton, who was the number one choice, and Alan Rough, who was nearing the end of his Scotland career but who I still expected to be ahead of me in the pecking order. We all worked together under the supervision of the Aberdeen trainer Teddy Scott. It was a revelation for me to see how differently Jim and Roughie approached goalkeeping. You could not get a greater contrast. Jim was very serious about his job – he still is – while Roughie was more like myself in that he was happy-go-lucky and very laid back. As a young keeper with very little experience, it was fascinating just to watch and listen to them.

I suppose because I was closer to Roughie in temperament I was able to identify with him better at that time – and later too, when I joined Hibs and he was still at Easter Road. He made mistakes in his career and people will keep bringing them up, but he won 50-odd caps for Scotland and he saved Hibs from relegation almost single-handedly one season. What I learned from watching him was how to be single-minded when you go out there on to the pitch. When you looked at him you would be forgiven for thinking he didn't have a care in the world. Nothing would faze him and not a single thing was allowed to intrude. He acted as if he didn't have a single nerve in his body. If he made a mistake, he would push it to the back of his mind and get on with the rest of the game, always remaining focused. Roughie taught me that it's not the mistakes you make that you should worry about, it's how you get over the mistakes and how you recover from them. That is the really testing time for any goalkeeper at any level, because it is after you make a blunder that you are placed under the miscroscope and your game is analysed. The error you made is shown again and again and again on television and you cannot let that affect you. If you do then your confidence goes and your entire game will very likely go with it. It's always been said that being a goalkeeper is the loneliest position on the field and you certainly learn that when you screw up because there's no hiding place for you. But Roughie had that one right. He just tucked it all away for future reference and was never found lacking in bottle.

Jim was different but he had similar qualities. He had the same determination and the same strength, his problems at Manchester United and then at Dundee proving that he can fight back from any kind of adversity. His comeback, after all the anguish he suffered, is one of the great stories in Scottish soccer, and the way he clawed his way back to the top with Hibs and Scotland is an example to anyone coming into the game. There is a very serious side to Jim, and believe it or not, he was the first guy I ever worked with who talked about the technique of keeping goal. The first one. Before training with Jim I thought I could just go out there and play without having to put any thought into it whatsoever. I would just get out, make a few saves and try not to lose too many goals. I had been playing cricket regularly too and the co-ordination which helped me in both games was something that came easily to me. Working with Jim was a revelation. He looked into his own game and he examined the way other goalkeepers approached certain situations. He would analyse the saves he made and the goals he lost. I had never experienced anything like this thoroughness. He wanted to talk about the different things you could experience in a game; about cross balls, coming off your line to narrow angles, or trying to force a forward into shooting for goal before he was ready to do so. To begin with, I couldn't make much of a contribution at all. 'What do you think?' he would ask. Or, 'How would you approach that?' And I didn't really have a clue. All I did know was that I was nowhere near the standard of Jim Leighton and I didn't have a fraction of his experience or technical knowledge, so I found myself struggling to take any real part in the discussions which Jim instigated. A few years down the line, I now realise that Jim was wondering how I would react in case he could pick up anything from my approach because that is how we all work. We take a little bit here and a little bit there and then hope that we can put it all together and produce a style of goalkeeping which suits our own particular needs. Jim must have wondered just what kind of a guy I was because I had so little to say on the subject. I suddenly recognised that technique was something I would have to learn about if I wanted to improve my game, and that it was only by practising the same way as Jim did and analysing everything about my game, that I would ever realise my full potential as a goalkeeper. Fortunately, the next season Alan Hodgkinson arrived at Oldham and my formal education into the mysteries of my chosen position began.

Not that it came easily. While everyone in the game knows that Hodgy has been my goalkeeping guru for a dozen years or so, the relationship did not get off to any kind of auspicious start. When Alan Hodgkinson arrived at Boundary Park at the request of Joe Royle, it was definitely not love at first sight.

Until then I hadn't been asked to work on the technical aspects of the job. I trained with the rest of the players and went into goal to stop shots and cut out cross balls, but nothing more. Whenever I gave away a soft goal, I wouldn't be able to explain what I had done wrong. Big Joe would come into the dressing room and ask, 'What the hell did you think you were doing out there?', and I couldn't really tell him. I would attempt to explain my view of the goal to him and then he would come back and ask me if I would do the same if that particular set of circumstances arose again. We would get ourselves into an argument when neither of us really knew what we were talking about. Sometimes I would accept his view and when a similar ball came in I would deal with it in the way he suggested, maybe adding a little bit of my own thing. Literally, quite literally, I was learning from my mistakes, and that clearly wasn't good enough. Joe knew that before I did. Essentially I was self taught and while that had carried me into the Scotland set-up there was no guarantee that I would progress much further unless I began to work harder on the technical aspects of the game. So Joe sent for Hodgy and everything began to change for the better, although the learning process was gradual.

For the first few weeks, I didn't see how the different training routines were going to help me. In fact, it got so bad that I went to Joe Royle and suggested that he should get rid of Alan because I just could not work with him. I really couldn't figure out where Hodgy was trying to take me. Apart from the few weeks' experience in the States and Mexico watching Jim Leighton, this was all new to me and I wasn't comfortable with it. I thought it was a waste of time for me and a waste of money for the club, but Joe asked if I would let it go for another couple of weeks and then take it from there. I agreed, even though I couldn't see my feelings changing in that time. To some extent I had closed my mind to all the new ideas which were being put forward to make me a better and more professional footballer. I just thought I knew better.

I was wrong. And inside that two weeks, thankfully, I

discovered my mistake and Alan Hodgkinson opened my eyes to the real world of goalkeeping. He has been opening my eyes ever since. It all came right for me in a game we played – against Fulham, I think – during the 'trial period' Joe had suggested. In training Hodgy had been asking me to look at a couple of situations and had advised me on how I should deal with them whenever they came up in an actual game. They came up this time. Not once but twice. Two incidents which we had looked at and worked on in training happened in the same 90 minutes and I took Alan's advice and made saves which I might not have made without his guidance. And there I was – a convert! I can actually remember saying to myself the first time, 'Hang on, what are you doing in this position?' because there I was taking up the position Hodgy had advised without even knowing what I was doing. It worked – and that was the real beginning of my career.

Basically his credo is simple: he tells you to look at where you were positioned when you lost a goal and then ask yourself if you could have been better placed. He always asks you if there was anything you could have done better. He has lived by that in his own career as goalkeeper and he wants us to live by the same code. He makes you look at the various things which happened in a game and eventually you start to think that if you had been a foot one way or the other then it might have made all the difference. The next time it happens you make the alteration in your approach and you make a save, knowing that all the work and thought and self-analysis have paid off.

I think the fact that I am looked on as being small for a keeper – I'm five feet eleven inches, by the way – has allowed us to form a special bond because when Hodgy played he was looked on as being too small as well. Yet he played in the English First Division for 22 years, as well as playing for England, and a contemporary of his, Eddie Hopkinson, also played for England despite being considered not tall enough. Goalies are all expected to be six feet plus. The lack of that extra inch or two does expose you to the odd snide remark, but Hodgy went through them before I had to and most of the work he does with me is about the movement of your feet and how important that can be to carry you up to that top corner of the goal. I can't do that from a standing jump, so it's a question of getting your feet right as you move across the goal and then making your jump. You have to be able to get up there so you work at that part of your game. If you concentrate hard enough you can overcome any of the supposed deficiencies and, at the same time, if you continue to work on what you are good at then your game comes into a sharper, more defined focus. It's funny how Hodgy concentrated on the things where I had problems – again the height thing comes into that – but at Easter Road Peter McCloy wanted most of the work to be done low, around your feet. I think that was probably because he was around six feet four inches, and while he could make the high balls from a standing jump quite easily he was worried about the low ones. So I learned one aspect of the game from Alan Hodgkinson and then another from Peter McCloy – and you discard nothing until you work out what is right for you. Gradually, all the pieces of the jigsaw fit together.

Eventually you become the finished article. You become your own man. It would be easy to say I wanted to be like Peter Shilton or Jim Leighton or Ray Clemence but I couldn't be like any of them. What you can do is take a little bit here and a little bit there and apply it to your own game. Hodgy used to say to me, 'Take it and try it. But if it doesn't feel right, if you're not comfortable with whatever you happen to be trying, then get rid of it,' and that's how I have tried to work. In fact, when I survey my career I wonder how I managed to do anything without his guidance and I sure as hell don't know what I would do without him now. He's always there when I need him and always has an answer for whatever goalkeeping problem you might come up with. He also makes sure that you don't allow your standards to drop. If he senses any lessening in your professional approach, he is on you like a ton of bricks. Nothing escapes him. I only wish he had been around when I first joined Rangers because, while that had been the place I wanted to be and the goalkeeping position I hoped to fit into, I had a very bad beginning. And when things started to go wrong for me I suddenly realised that keeping goal for Rangers wasn't going to be the easy job I had anticipated. I had watched Chris Woods in the Rangers goal and seen him being asked to make just four or five saves in almost every game they played because they were just so much on top in the normal run of Premier League matches. And I used to think that would do me just fine: nice lazy afternoons.

I couldn't have been more wrong. Maybe it was just that Woodsy made it look easy but when I got there and was moved into the firing line, it only took the first half-dozen games or so of the season to open my eyes to the incredible pressure which attaches itself to every player at the club. And of course I had to find out the hard way. So hard was it that at the time I began to wish that I had not taken the opportunity to join up at Ibrox and simply opted to stay with Hibs.

My old manager at Hibs, Alex Miller, had spent all his playing career at Ibrox and he had warned me about what was expected from the players and the high standards which were set. While I took his advice on board, I did have the feeling that there was a bit of mystique about the club which wasn't exactly appropriate to the modern game. The shock that was in store for me came early in one of the pre-season training sessions when I was doing a 25-minute run in Bellahouston Park – the kind I can't do any more and even back then didn't relish. A distance runner I was not.

The rest of the players were just about out of sight as I floundered in their wake and manager Walter Smith ran alongside me and gave me a hard time for not being able to keep up. Being the new boy, and trying to live up to my Jack-the-lad reputation, I said, 'If you wanted to sign a runner then you should have gone for Seb Coe.' I knew right away that making a joke like this was a mistake. A near-fatal mistake. When the training session was over I was told the gaffer wanted to see me: it was my first trip up the 'marbles' and the first time I found out how hard a man Walter Smith can be.

He laid it right on the line for me. There was no beating about the bush. I had to lose a stone in weight during the pre-season stint at Il Ciocco, the Italian training camp, or he would keep Chris Woods and sell me on. Woodsy was still there, of course, and I knew Walter meant what he said. Here I was just five minutes at the club and already in trouble. I would have to knuckle down and lose the weight. Walter went on to explain what was expected from players at the club, emphasising the level of commitment required from every single player. There were no half measures from the gaffer that day. I knew that I had to go to Italy and train harder than I had ever done before otherwise my career at the club could be over before it had even begun.

I did work hard. I trained like a beast. The weight came off and I started the season as the first-team goalkeeper – and if I thought I had troubles pre-season then they were nothing compared to what hit me in the opening weeks of that first year with the club.

We won the first two games of that 1991–92 season comfortably with a six-goal hammering of St Johnstone in the opener and then a follow-up 2-0 win over Motherwell with both games at Ibrox. So there I was with no goals lost and going back to Edinburgh to face Hearts in the third match. That's when I conceded my first goal and it was a bad one. Even now I can visualise the way it happened. The ball was knocked in from our left and with the benefit of hindsight I realise now that my standing position was not too great. I had been waiting for the Hearts player to knock the ball into the penalty box but instead he sent it to Scott Crabbe. I took a look around the penalty box to see where he might put it but instead of playing a pass he shot. There was still a bit of spin on the ball when he made contact with it and it was one of those high dropping ones which are always difficult for any goalkeeper. I made it harder for myself, though, by believing that the ball was going to fly wide. As soon as you do that you seem to freeze; you just can't move your feet. The same thing happened in the Scottish Cup semi-final last season when Falkirk drew with Celtic in the first match – they went on to beat them, of course – and young Stewart Kerr was caught the same way and tried to explain it afterwards. I had sympathy for him when he admitted that he had been unable to move his feet because any goalkeeper will tell you that this can happen. It certainly hit me at Tynecastle that afternoon. I had convinced myself the ball was off target so there was just no response when I realised that I was going to be wrong. I'm looking at this ball coming through the air towards me and it's getting closer and closer. I reckon it was only a couple of yards from me when it went into the net. I knew that I could and should have saved it but I was rooted to the line. I couldn't even make a move when my mind told me I had misjudged the shot. This shot was not going wide. This shot was going into the net and I was going to get the blame. I could not believe what had happened, but the goal was scored, the game was lost and the knives were out for me. I was slaughtered by the press. It was a shocking goal to lose and I knew that better than any of my critics. What I didn't realise, even though I knew the club was high profile, was that the reaction to the goal and the defeat would be so great. It was just so far removed from anything I had ever had to experience before. I had always been under pressure at Hibs and seen a lot of action but if I lost a goal then it was often expected and people generally made far more of the saves I had to make than the goals I let in. It was usually the case that I had to make a dozen or so saves a game. This was a whole new scenario; a situation where I was asked to make only two or three stops a game so that a mistake was immediately put under the spotlight. One bad goal lost was looked on as a major tragedy. Worse was to come and my natural confidence was being eroded all the time. I was learning the hard way that what Alex Miller had warned me of – the pressure which is heaped on players at Ibrox by the demands of the support – had not been exaggerated. You had to be strong to stand up to this and I had to find that inner strength to carry me through. I don't know how I did it because it did come close to destroying me, despite the fact that I have never been the kind of footballer who carries his worries around with him. I always take the view that what has happened cannot be undone and you simply must get on, learn from the mistake and do better the next time. It's the way I have always been and it's the same message Hodgy preaches.

Only Hodgy was not yet in place at Ibrox. There was no goalkeeping coach around, no shoulder for me to cry on, and I had to take the brunt of the blame on my own shoulders. And if I thought the reaction after the Tynecastle blunder was bad then within the next few weeks I found that there was no hiding place for a Rangers goalkeeper when he makes errors of judgement.

We were able to recover in the League by beating Celtic 2-0 at Parkhead in the first Old Firm match of the season, but a couple of weeks later we lost 1-0 to Sparta Prague in our opening European Cup game in Czechoslovakia. Again, it was a goal which I felt I should have saved. Over the 90 minutes I had done well but when they scored I felt I could have done better. In fairness, it was one of those goals which any keeper can lose. In fact, I can remember Chris Woods playing for Rangers in a Scottish Cup game against Dunfermline and losing one very similar. It was the kind of shot which might have been meant as a cross and as it came in from the right I felt I had positioned myself properly. Yet it sailed over my head and into the net and that was the one goal of the game. It looked bad – that kind of goal always does – but it wasn't as bad a mistake as the one at Tynecastle. When placed together, though, the two goals brought me harsh criticism from the newspapers. There were suggestions that Walter had made a mistake in splashing out a million pounds to buy me when he had Woodsy in place. It was not the best of times for me because I wasn't used to criticism. At my two previous clubs I had always been a bit of a hero to the supporters and I had always had a good press.

And still the nightmare did not end. A week later we lost to my old club Hibs in the semi-final of the League Cup at Hampden and I found myself out of my first competition with Rangers, with my old mates heading towards what turned out to be their first trophy win in many years.

Another week on and it was the return game against Sparta, a match we were convinced we would win. We did, too, but not by a big enough margin, and once more a bad, late goal cost us our place alongside the major clubs in the next stage of the tournament. Stuart McCall had scored to level the tie on aggregate but no matter how hard we tried we couldn't break down the Czech defence for the second goal we needed. The game moved into extra time and Stuart struck again. Then, with the minutes ticking away, that position we wanted among Europe's elite was snatched from us right at the death. Sparta made one of their few breaks forward towards the end of extra time and one of their players placed a ball between myself and Scott Nisbet. These are never the best to deal with, and as Nissy followed the ball back into the box he believed there was a Czech player behind him, snapping at his heels and ready to make a challenge for the ball. In actual fact, none of the opposition were close to him at all but he decided to play safe and slid in to play the ball back towards goal. The ball was now coming back to me, about a yard or so to my right, and I knew I could still get to it OK even after he had touched it. Then what happened? It took a bad bounce right in front of me, just enough to carry it out of my reach.

It went over my shoulder and into the net and that one goal was enough to send Sparta onward in the competition and leave me facing the wrath of the manager. I was devastated when I got into the dressing room and I didn't know what to expect. The ball *had* bounced badly, but I knew I couldn't hide behind that. As I was sitting there, head hung low, the dressing-room door burst open and the gaffer stormed in. I have never seen him as angry as he was that night. For a moment I thought he was going to belt me one. He was right up in my face, nose to nose, and then he gave me the biggest roasting I have ever had as a player.

I can remember his words now. 'You told everyone you wanted to come here and that you wanted to play at the very top level. That's what you were quoted as saying when you signed. Well, you're here, you're at the top level and look what you've just done! I would have been better keeping the other fellow!' That's how scathing he was, and I just took it because there was nothing else I could do. I knew how disastrous the loss of that late goal was for the club and I realised, too, that for the first time in my career there were question marks being put alongside my performances. Nothing I had done with Oldham or Hibs or even on the international stage with Scotland mattered any more. I had to prove myself good enough to be the Rangers goalkeeper. I had to show that I had the character to come back from the mistakes I had made and then demonstrate why the club had bought me in the first place.

The other thing I had to do was convince the dressing room that I could handle the pressures which came with the job. It's a hard school in there and I knew that I would never be one of the lads until I had proved myself all over again. I had been able to show what I could do when I was playing *against* Rangers; now I had to show just what I could do when I was playing *for* them. To make things even more difficult for me, I knew the players were seeing my mistakes and wondering if I was ever going to be able to match up to Chris Woods. With Chris, who had been with the club for a few seasons, they had won just about everything. They all had confidence in him and here I was, in the team to try to take over his role, messing things up. Quite honestly, just a few months into my new life as a Rangers player, I simply didn't know where to turn or what to do. I think some of the lads had probably made up their minds and decided that I wasn't going to be able to do the job. At one point I was so low I thought about phoning Joe Royle and asking him to get me out of the whole sorry mess. That's the kind of blind panic I found myself in. I knew Joe had wanted to take me back to Boundary Park when Oldham moved into the First Division and the thought of being wanted was enough to colour my thoughts. I felt so vulnerable, I would have walked away from the club I had wanted to play for most of all and gone back down to England. I had little confidence left and I really didn't know if I was ever going to be able to become accustomed to the pressure which the other Ibrox players had known and lived with over the seasons they had been at the club. I knew there was no one who could help me through this; I had to do it on my own and hope that I would emerge from this personal crisis as a better goalkeeper. The problem was that I wasn't sure if I could ever recover from the disastrous start which had shattered my self-belief and the belief of other players. The next game was against Airdrie at Broomfield and by this time I didn't even want to go out on to the field, knowing that I would be scrutinised yet again. When I was selected I went into the game hoping I wouldn't have to touch the ball throughout the 90 minutes, and I'd never felt like that before. I was in such a state I didn't even want to see the ball in our half of the field. Throughout the game – and I find this hard to believe now – I muttered away to myself on the goal line: 'Don't shoot'; 'Please don't cross the ball'; 'Just keep the ball away from me, for God's sake'. And when my own defenders had the ball I was telling them not to pass it back but just get it up the field.

All I wanted was to get through the 90 minutes without making a mistake. We won 4-0, there was no mistake and I survived. Maybe that was kind of a turning point because since then I have never known a spell like that one. I still remember sitting at home with Tracy, discussing the whole thing and wondering if I had made the right move. Deep down I knew I had but the goals I had lost had brought it home to me just how intense the pressure is on Rangers players and how severe the public scrutiny can be. The glare of publicity was rarely shone on Boundary Park or Easter Road and even on the odd occasions when it was, there was never the same ferocity about it as there was day in and day out at Ibrox. As for the actual playing side itself, that was a whole lot different too. I had to contend with long, long spells of inactivity because Rangers, of course, always had so much of the play in the games we took part in, especially in the Premier League. It's easy to allow your concentration to lapse when you're having very little to do in the way of saves. If you let your guard down for just one single moment, it could be enough to lose a cup or the League or have the team knocked out of Europe. That's the tightrope you walk game after game, week after week, season after season. And as I discovered, you have to adjust to it swiftly if you are going to survive. I found that out very soon and realised that the lazy afternoons I had envisaged were nothing of the kind. They contained far too much menace.

My predecessor, Chris Woods, had this kind of goal-keeping down to a fine art. He would be there in goal, doing nothing for maybe 40 minutes or more, and then he would be asked to cut out a cross or stop a shot, or leave his line to cut down the angle on an attacking player. Because he was so tremendously focused he was able to do that. The gaffer talked to me about that aspect of the job because he knew it was so different for me; I was so accustomed to being in action all the time. Learning to concentrate even when the ball is at the other end of the pitch isn't something anyone can teach you. It's not like technique, which you can have demonstrated to you and then learn from what you have seen. It is a discipline you must work out on your own. I accept that I have had my off-field problems, most of them well known to the rest of the country, but I never allow them to affect my job. While it took time to adapt at Ibrox, I did have the capacity for concentration which the job requires. Whenever I cross that white line I have tunnel vision. All I focus on is the game; what is happening out there in front of me. There is no question about it: I know that I have to be in control of the situation, especially the area immediately around my goal, and that is what I have always tried to do after those early bloomers.

Playing in goal is a specialist job and I don't think any of the other players can properly relate to what we have to do. That's why we hang around together, either at club or international level, even where there are elements of rivalry involved. You can be chasing the same position but you still work together. When I arrived at Ibrox, Woodsy was still there, and while there had been suggestions that he was unhappy about my being bought the issue never surfaced between us at training. The season before I signed, Chris had told the gaffer that he wanted to leave, despite the fact that the press claimed that Rangers had signed me from Hibs behind his back. It was never like that. Woodsy knew as well as anyone that the limitations of the 'three foreigners' rule made it difficult for Rangers to keep an English keeper. It meant that they could then use only two more 'foreign' players for their club competitions and that was not ideal. By signing me from Hibs that pressure was eased and the way was open for three outfield players to be deployed.

Woodsy was fine with me and we trained together for the short spell he remained with Rangers until he was transferred. He gave me advice when he thought I needed it and I found working with him instructive. He was a big fellow, and for someone as tall and powerfully built as he was he had amazing reactions. I was always impressed that he worked hardest on what he was good at, forever trying to improve. There was no animosity between us, although I know supporters will find that difficult to understand. It has been the same in the Scotland set-up for a long, long time now. While you feel lousy if you are left out – as I did in Italy at the World Cup and as Jim Leighton did in England at the European Championship finals – you put that aside and get on with helping the other keeper prepare for the games. It's just the way goalkeepers are with each other. Only goalkeepers can understand goalkeepers. We are a breed apart and I think the bond exists because our job is so different from that of the other players in the team. We are on our own out there a lot of the time and when we make a mistake, it's usually a vital one. That's a lot of responsibility to shoulder.

Other players can miss a tackle in midfield, or even in defence, and a forward can fail to put in a proper cross, but these are forgotten. If we slip up, there is usually a goal lost and everyone remembers that. Perhaps that explains why we're all supposed to be a bit crazy, although there are a couple of exceptions – my Scotland mate Jim Leighton and my one-time Old Firm rival Pat Bonner of Celtic.

Big Packy is one of the nicest fellows you could meet in

the game and I have good reasons for saying that. It was after the disaster I'd had against Hearts that he helped me out with some advice. At the end of my very first Old Firm game at Celtic Park, which we had won 2-0, Packy shook my hand and said he would like to have a word with me in the players' lounge once we had changed. I thought he wanted to talk goalkeepers' gloves or something equally as trivial, but he actually wanted to tell me about the peculiar and probably unique pressure of playing in goal for one of the Old Firm clubs and how I could cope with it. It was one of the kindest gestures I have ever witnessed in all my years in the game. I just wish that some of the fans – some of those who can't see any good at all when they look across the great divide which separates the two Glasgow giants – could have been there to see Pat Bonner giving me advice and encouragement at the very beginning of my Rangers career. It certainly put a different perspective on the whole business.

Bonner told me to ignore everyone who was having a go at me, stop reading the newspapers and stop speaking to the press for a couple of months or so. That way, he explained, things would settle down and I would get back to the important aspects of keeping goal, which meant focusing only on the job itself. That, he added, was hard enough for any goalkeeper because of the spotlight which shines on the Old Firm. I knew I was getting a lesson from someone who had been over this complicated course and knew the pitfalls; someone who had suffered as I was suffering. I took his words on board, and they helped me through many a difficult time. I stayed out of the limelight, I didn't talk to the press (apart from one or two friends there), and I tried to divorce myself from the various off-field worries and concentrate wholly on the job I had to do. Nothing else, I told myself, mattered. From that day on I have followed the sound advice he gave me and I have retained enormous respect for Pat Bonner as a man.

Jim Leighton, too, has been a gentleman to me through the years we have been together in the Scotland squad. These two don't really qualify for the goalies' club. They are both far too intelligent – and their records speak for their ability. It's funny how so many disparate personalities can still share the same problems and the same worries and it's lucky we can talk each other through the hard times. It can get lonely, being a goalkeeper, but there is a common bond between us all that the centre forwards, say, haven't got. No one else understands us because no one else can appreciate what it means to lose a bad goal and hear the crowd baying for you. It's always been said that there is no hiding place for the goalkeeper and we all know that. We work together. We laugh together. We suffer together.

The Guru on the Goalie –
Alan Hodgkinson Analyses
Andy Goram

T HE MOST IMPORTANT thing about Andy Goram's goal-keeping is the very high level of technique he has managed to achieve over the years. Indeed, I don't think there is any other goalkeeper in world football better than Andy as far as pure technique is concerned. That has been his forte and it is not a target he has reached without hours and hours of hard work on the training ground. That's where Andy Goram has been able to turn himself into one of the best goalkeepers in Europe, despite the handicap of size which many people thought he wouldn't be able to overcome. It is to his credit that he never allowed that to discourage him at all, nor has it affected his play.

Obviously he has made up for his lack of height in many different ways: his marvellous positional sense, his bravery and the expert timing he displays in catching and holding the ball. He is, basically, a goalkeeper who never gives away bad goals and that is a very important attribute in any keeper who aspires to be world class. Andy doesn't make bad mistakes. You don't see him, for instance, fumbling shots and letting the ball run loose so that players can rush in and knock the ball into the net. That stems from hard work; he has made sure that he gets and holds the ball. Once he has it he won't let it slip from his grasp carelessly. I am genuinely delighted that I have been able to work with him all these years and watch him progress from a raw – and I mean raw – youngster into the master goalkeeper he has become.

I can still remember when we started out together and I think we both thought it was a mistake. We certainly didn't hit it off. I have to admit I wasn't convinced about Andy, and he didn't understand what I was trying to teach him because until we started our training routines he had simply been teaching himself as he went along – though Oldham manager Joe Royle had recognised even in that self-learning period that there was a real talent. So much so that he had rung me umpteen times and asked me to work with Andy. I can still remember him saying, 'Come and work with this keeper I've got. You have to come because he's going to be the best goalkeeper in the world but he needs some guidance and I can't give him that.'

But at that particular time my diary was full. I was so busy working with other goalkeepers that there was no way I could fit Oldham and Andy Goram into my schedule.

The first time I clapped eyes on him in action I couldn't see what the fuss was about. By this time Joe had been on the phone to me again and I knew that I would eventually have to take a look at this goalkeeper he was talking about. So I went to see him in the Oldham Reserves when they played one night at Coventry. Andy was just coming back from injury, which was why he was in the second string. I can be forgiven for wondering what it was this goalkeeper possessed that made Joe Royle rave about him because the Oldham Reserves lost 8-0 that night. At the end of the game Joe tapped me on the shoulder and told me, 'Honest, Alan, that was not the real Andy Goram out there. He's coming back from injury and that's what made him look bad. Please, don't judge him on tonight's game.'

As luck would have it, I went to Oldham the next season. A gap had appeared in my training schedules and I phoned Joe and explained that I was ready to start work with his lad.

The opening session did not go well. I started off by giving Andy and the other goalkeepers who were at the club a talk about the importance of good technique and, to be perfectly honest, Andy didn't have a clue what I was trying to tell him. He didn't understand anything about the technical side of goalkeeping, which makes his status now even more amazing. I set out a few routines for them to work at and when Andy just couldn't get one of them right, he turned and booted the ball to the other end of the training ground in sheer frustration. I ignored it because the other lads were still concentrating on the tasks I had set them, but when they'd finished I said to him, 'You see that ball down there, the one you kicked away, off you go and fetch it back.' Then I added, 'In fact, just run down there and get it!' He looked at me in a kind of surprised way and then gave me another look as if to say there was no way he was going to do what I told him. But I knew that I couldn't afford to back off in this one so I said, 'Either you go down there and fetch that ball back or you go into the dressing room and we're finished.' Maybe it was something he saw in me at that moment because he turned and he went and he got the ball. I think I had his respect from that moment on.

I did wonder, though, what I was taking on for Joe. Going back home that day I was convinced that Andy was a hooligan. I was wrong. He was a bit impulsive and a bit daft – but then all of us goalkeepers are a bit daft according to legend – yet he was also to become the hardest-working goalkeeper I have been involved with. I suppose there is an affinity between us because just as Andy has been described as being too small for a top-class keeper, I too had my own share of that when I was playing. I'm around the same height as Andy and I played for England and was a professional for a good many years. I had to work to overcome any deficiency which might have been there and so I had certain training programmes which were designed to offset any lack of inches. There was lots of agility work and positional work – placing of your feet and that kind of thing – and this is what I have refined over the years and what I have asked Andy to do in the time I have been associated with him. In effect, the problems caused by being a few inches short of what most goalkeepers are in terms of height are overcome by the development of technique. I discovered that as a player and Andy discovered that as well. He also learnt that to be at the top and to stay at the top you have to be consistent.

I'm not talking about consistency over a period of five or six games; I'm referring to the kind of consistency which Andy has shown week after week, month after month and season after season. I have never known any other goalkeeper maintain such high standards over such a long period of time. What helps him, too, is his nature. He is genuinely hurt when he loses a goal or when the team loses a game. He doesn't like that one little bit. In fact, his attitude can't be bettered. He hates to lose.

That is demonstrated perfectly in the way he stands up to opposing players when they are coming in on goal. He is the best in the world at standing up when he is in that one-on-one situation. I watch him doing it when I'm at the game and I'll watch it again on television later and, honestly, I have never seen any keeper do it better. And if I've been able to help him do that, then I've done a good job. He stays up better than anyone else and he just stares down the forward who happens to be against him. What he does is transfer the pressure from himself to the striker. Suddenly, because he has stood up, the goal begins to look smaller and smaller to the man on the ball and invariably the forward makes a mistake in his finishing. It's there that you see the art in Andy Goram's goalkeeping style.

It is not something that has come easily to him. Certainly he had natural attributes which he brought with him and which he had back when I first knew him at Oldham. These were the things Joe Royle saw in him – the eye and hand co-ordination and the courage, for example. You don't teach them. They came with the territory! You just have to remember that Andy was also a Scottish international at cricket to realise that he has a born gift for ball games of all kinds, not just football. But the kind of goalkeeper he has become has not come naturally. It has been intellectually acquired, if you like, because he has worked harder than any other keeper I know to master his job. He had to learn that it's not only about catching the ball; it's also about positioning yourself for any ball which comes in on goal. First of all he resisted the lessons I was giving him. It was only when he realised that he was improving that he began to work the way I hoped he would.

Too many people get the wrong idea about Andy Goram because of some of the off-field antics he has been linked with. They don't count as far as I'm concerned, because on the training ground where I see him he is utterly focused on what we have to do there. It is the work he does which allows him to set these consistently high standards – and they are tremendously high. I work with Peter Schmeichel at Manchester United, David Seaman at Arsenal and Neville Southall at Everton and over the years Andy is right up there alongside them in general all-round performances and ahead of any of them on technical ability.

The only disappointment is that he hasn't won 50 caps for Scotland. He should have. And he would have if it hadn't been for the terrible run of injuries he has suffered since the treble-winning season. One major piece of surgery which was done in the United States and then several minor operations have interrupted his career. It says a lot for his personal courage that he has fought back each time and returned to play as well as ever.

I can tell you a wonderful story about how Andy became the Scotland goalkeeper when he might have been capped by England, meaning that the Scots would have lost one of the best international goalies they have ever had. Andy had been selected, along with Gary Bailey of Manchester United, for an England Under 21 team who were playing against Bulgaria at Portsmouth. I will always remember the phone call I received before that game. It was from the manager of the England side and he was saying to me: 'Alan, I don't have a goalkeeper for this game. Gary Bailey has gone and got himself injured and he can't play and I've just had a training session with Andy Goram and I can't go into the game with him because he's hopeless.'

I spent a lot of time trying to convince him he was making a mistake about Andy but there was no budging him. He just wasn't for playing Andy at all, so I eventually suggested to him that he bring in a fellow called Alan Knight, who was with Portsmouth. He could be the over-age player and being a local he was likely to bring in a few more fans to Fratton Park. So that's the solution he went for and Andy was left out, which led to him eventually getting his chance with Scotland. Although Andy was probably disappointed about England at the time, things really couldn't have worked out better, especially because I became a member of Andy Roxburgh's and then Craig Brown's backroom staff.

However, fast forward a few seasons after that and by this time, as well as helping with Scotland I'm also with Glasgow Rangers, who are playing Leeds United in the European Cup. They beat them twice. The first time they won at Ibrox and then at Elland Road in the return they repeated the 2-1 win and Andy Goram had a wonderful night. He was superb and Leeds could not find a way past him no matter what they tried. I was so pleased afterwards because Andy had proved an important point to the manager of England's Under 21 team all these years before. The team boss then had been Howard Wilkinson, manager of Leeds, whose heart Andy had broken.

I think he also proved a lot of commentators wrong

that night. Contrary to popular opinion, there is a high standard among the keepers north of the Border and he certainly demonstrated that against Leeds. Jim Leighton has also shown what he can do, even after the traumatic times he went through.

It has been a privilege for me to work with Andy and it's a matter of great professional pride to me when he insists on handing me some of the credit for what he has done. I can only hand a great deal of it back to him. While I could put the work routines in place, it required someone with a totally professional and focused approach to goalkeeping to be able to combine it with his own natural attributes. I don't think you will find a goalkeeper anywhere who would disagree with me when I argue that he is technically the best in the business. Other keepers see something in Andy that supporters and even other players can't always see. They are able to appreciate just what he has been able to do and what he has continued to do in so many important games. It's significant that when he did lose a bad goal last season there was a tremendous fuss made about it in the Scottish newspapers. That's because no one could quite believe that Andy was able to let in the goal he had lost against Aberdeen at Pittodrie. I suppose it proved that the occasional nightmare can hit even the most infallible goalkeepers. Knowing Andy, though, I'm sure he spent a lot of time afterwards telling himself never to make that mistake again. And he won't!

7 Euro 96 and My First Wembley

IT SEEMED TO BE FATED that we would be drawn in the same group as England for the finals of the European Championship. Throughout the qualifying games against Russia, Greece, Finland, San Marino and the Faeroe Islands, the Tartan Army had been chanting 'Wembelee, Wembelee, Wembelee', even though there was no guarantee that Scotland would ever play there unless we actually reached the final itself.

Yet the fans sang on: their destination was Wembley and nothing less was going to satisfy them. Of course, the great London ground has long held a special place in Scotland's footballing folklore. When the British Championship games were being played regularly it was always the game at Wembley against England which dominated all the others. Indeed, until these games were abandoned, it often meant more to the Scottish supporters than the World Cup games which gradually superseded the British matches in importance. Every second year there was a pilgrimage to London and the tales of Wembley weekends are the very stuff of Tartan Army legend. Now, of course, the supporters have more exotic locations they can talk about. They have been at major tournament finals from West Germany to Argentina, Spain to Italy and Mexico to Sweden – countries that previous generations had not believed would ever be in reach. As the World Cup and the European Championship grew in importance, the

British matches inevitably faded away and the annual clashes with England disappeared, reappearing sporadically for the Sir Stanley Rous Trophy and then vanishing altogether. Funnily enough, during the build-up to the European finals, Terry Venables and Craig Brown had talked about the possibility of resurrecting the regular meetings, but nothing came of it because the football authorities and the police were worried about possible trouble. Then came the draw – and we were going to Wembley to face England in our second competitive game of the finals. It was as if the Tartan Army had sensed what was going to happen. For eighteen months they had set their hearts on a Wembley return and here it was, in a fiercely competitive situation.

No one had really expected Scotland to go through from the qualifying group but Craig Brown had always been confident. As he kept stressing, 'We don't want to see a party going on next door and find that we haven't earned an invitation.' That had happened in 1966 and he didn't want it to happen again. It made the lads more determined than ever that they would be there – yet we were in the same group as the Russians, who are always formidable. Then there were the Greeks, who had been at the World Cup finals in the United States in 1994. While they hadn't done particularly well once they reached that stage, they had at least qualified, which was one step further than us. At club level they were making good progress too, as we had found out to our cost at Ibrox when AEK beat us in the preliminary round of the European Champions' League.

So, while Craig made confident noises and our determination grew, we did all realise that this was no walkover. If we were to qualify we would have to do so with some strong results and we couldn't afford to lose to any of the weaker nations. In the event, we did just that. The key result was the opening group win against Finland in Helsinki, allowing us to feel more confident about the task which lay ahead. Then two draws against Russia, home and away, and just a solitary defeat from Greece in Athens, when the referee decided Colin Hendry had fouled one of their players in the penalty box. Television showed clearly that it had not been a foul, but they scored and won the game. Then, and this is where the planning and attention to detail of the Scotland set-up comes into play, we had a run of five games at home against the Finns, the Greeks and the two weaker countries and we won all of them, going through to Euro 96 along with the Russians. It was a sustained performance from the group of players and even though I had been forced out of some of the games through injury, I was up for the finals like all the rest of the lads. The consistency shown by the team had been superb even though we still had to put up with a lot of criticism.

We are constantly being compared unfavourably with Scotland teams of the past, even though some of those so-called better teams don't have a record to match the one Craig has put together. Nor were they asked to play such formidable opposition. Sure, there are limitations in the team, but every team has its problems. Scotland have found it hard to replace Ally McCoist and even Mo Johnston, though he played on fewer occasions than Coisty. It's difficult when you lose natural goalscorers and Craig has tried all kinds of alternative combinations, although he was still able to get goals from Coisty in the qualifying games as well as in the finals. He scored a vital goal against Greece at Hampden and another against Switzerland at Villa Park, taking us closer and closer to the finals of a major tournament.

When that draw was made everything was dominated by the thought of playing England at Wembley. It was all the fans could talk about. The players were the same – very few had been to Wembley, and this was the game every Scottish schoolboy dreams about playing in. Now the chance had arrived and I was as excited as the next man.

But there were other considerations if we were going to be able to qualify for the quarter-finals – like playing Holland at Villa Park in the opening game. As always in these tournaments, the first match is vital. If you go into the finals and you fall at the first hurdle then you just don't have time to recover. You might be able to get back if you only have the weakest teams in the group left to play, but on this occasion we were going from Holland straight to the Wembley meeting with England. To make matters worse, we were going there without the full aid of the Tartan Army because the ticket allocation had been strictly limited. While we knew that a lot of our lads would make it into the English areas of the ground somehow or other, we also knew that they would be severely outnumbered on the day. And this was, after all, going in against the tournament hosts on the ground they knew best of all. Mind you, the Scottish Football Association were able to win a small off-field battle which amused all of us. Because the draw had made Scotland the home team, the SFA pointed out that we should occupy the home dressing room – which the European bosses ruled in our favour. After England had worked things out to their advantage by deciding to stick to Wembley for *all* their games, it was some kind of justice.

Still, the manager and his backroom staff all knew that Holland had to be handled first and to do that we all had to be in peak condition for this crucial game. Nothing less was going to satisfy them and there was no letting up. The lads who had not been playing regularly went to special training sessions at Inverclyde. No chances were being taken with the squad's fitness. I have to say that some of us did question this. It seemed strange to come off the back of a full season, having played around 50 highly competitive games, and work as hard as we had done when the season had begun back in August. Working in the heat in the States, particularly when we got down to Miami, wasn't the most pleasant way to prepare but the medical team and the rest of the backroom staff had things worked out so that we would go into the opening game at peak levels of fitness. All the work and preparations were aimed towards that match with the Dutch, even to the extent of abandoning Craig's favoured three-at-the-back defensive set-up to revert to a flat-back four. The manager was certain that Holland would use wingers and the best way to combat that was to play a more orthodox style at the back. We tried that out in the States and everyone fitted in OK, mainly, I suppose, because nearly all of the players were used to that system at club level. It was a bold move and a brave decision by the Scotland manager. He was the first of the British international team bosses to use the system which employs three central defenders and allows the full backs to operate further forward to become 'wing backs'; a system the players had enjoyed. It had been the base for the successes we had had in the qualifying games and yet he was ready to cast it aside and out-think the Dutch, who obviously believed that we could not and would not change at this late stage of the proceedings. They were wrong. And it was Craig Brown who was right on all counts.

He read the script correctly, in terms of the fitness required and the tactics the Dutch team would use against us. It required adjustments to be made to our style and it needed players to modify the way they usually played for their country. But the marvellous thing about the pool of players that Craig has put together is its versatility. The Celtic defender Tom Boyd can play in the three at the very heart of the defence or he can play in either of the full-back positions. Craig Burley from Chelsea is able to play at right back or in midfield but is especially effective in the wing-back role. Tosh McKinlay, another Celtic player, can also move into that attacking mode or remain as a more or less orthodox left back. And so it goes on. It allows the backroom staff to have various options open to them in all the games they play; they could even switch from one formation to another during a match because there are players who can simply slot into different positions without losing any of their effectiveness. It has been one of the strengths of the Brown era and I doubt that this will alter as long as Craig remains in charge of the international team. It is something he has worked on carefully and he knows it can work for him in terms of results and performances.

That's not to say we had an easy time in that first match. The opening twenty minutes had found me making one or two saves and thrown us back on the defensive. Gradually, though, as Craig had predicted, we began to get more of the ball and more of the game. We also found ourselves getting a little bit of luck, which I felt we had earned but I'm sure Holland would beg to differ. (I think we earned it because of the determination we showed against a powerful Dutch team who at that stage were among the favourites.) John Collins was guarding one of my posts when a ball struck him on the hand. The Dutch team appealed for a penalty but the referee waved play on and we survived. Not only did we hold out but we finished the stronger team. All the extra training in America, which had continued when we got to our Euro 96 headquarters at Stratford, had paid off. If we hadn't followed the carefully thought-out and well-planned regime, we would have died a death late in the match after absorbing all that pressure. Holland moved the ball around so well and yet, despite the way they attacked and kept on attacking us, didn't wear us down. We stood up to them, ended the game strongly and gained the psychological lift we needed. To lose would have been a terrible disappointment to endure before heading for the game at Wembley against the English.

Craig had always underlined just how much we needed that decent result first time out because no matter what happened at Wembley we all felt confident that we would be able to beat Switzerland in the final game, which could well decide qualification for the last eight. The match with the Swiss was the ace we felt we had up our sleeves. If we could go into that still looking good for a qualifying place then we felt we would be good enough to take out the team which had stopped us from going to the World Cup finals in the United States in 1994. That still rankled. We had had such a tremendous qualifying record in the game's number one tournament that it was a shock to us all when it finally came to an end – particularly when the Swiss were able to beat us to one of the top spots. We had felt we were better than they were back then and felt the same way now. Also, they had lost their influential coach, the Englishman Roy Hodgson, who had guided them through the World Cup qualifying section.

First, though, we had England and Wembley, the biggest occasion many of us had ever faced. I don't think I have ever had the same feelings before a game as I did that day. Even just the approach to Wembley was enough to put a lump in your throat, especially when we saw all the supporters there, expecting so much from the team and believing we could win the game and be the first Scotland team to progress to the later stages of a major football tournament. This was to be the year when we did that at last; the year when we defeated that jinx which had followed the country through one previous European Championship final and five World Cup finals. Many of us had only ever watched games between England and Scotland at Wembley on the box and now here we were, carrying the hopes of the nation and feeling the pressure. Fortunately there was a game staged beforehand with former players taking part, so we saw Gordon Strachan, Willie Donachie, John Wark and others which helped to relax us. But it wasn't easy to settle down and concentrate on the game rather than on all the factors which surrounded it.

But it had to be done as we sat in the dressing room and listened to Craig. England hadn't looked too convincing against the Swiss in their opening match and we all felt that the pressure of playing at home and the weight of expectation placed on players and manager alike by the English public and press was enormous. After the opener they had been pilloried, which worried us because they would be determined to bounce back to favour in this one against us. We knew they would be up for it but we knew we were ready as well. Craig had decided to go back to the normal defensive set-up because he recognised the menace England carried through the middle in the form of Alan Shearer, simply the best finisher in the tournament. But even knowing that, even being aware that he carried the biggest threat to us and to any other team England played in the tournament, we allowed him to score the first goal. Unusually for us, we were tactically slack at just the wrong moment and that was what allowed the Newcastle United frontman the opportunity to score and give them the lift they needed. Before the goal I thought we were doing OK; holding our own, using the ball cleverly and refusing to allow them to dominate as their fans demanded. When we were given a penalty in the second half it was the chance to haul ourselves back into the game. Instead, that minute and the one which followed proved to be the turning points of the game. We missed the penalty and then Paul Gascoigne scored England's second straight after Gary McAllister's miss. I can't think of many minutes in a game which hurt as much as those did. Even now I still replay that Gazza goal in my mind. I can still see him surging forward from the halfway line and bearing down on our goal. Colin Hendry was backing away from him and I was shouting, 'Stand up to him, stand up to him,' because after playing with him for a season I know that's the one way you might have a chance of stopping him when he's in that mode. Then he lofted the ball over his head and came into the box. I went out, so sure that he would hit the ball to the near post as I had seen him do so often in the past.

But of course he let me commit myself before sending it beyond me. I knew it was a goal. I knew without looking and I remember thinking, Not him, not Gazza, because I knew he would give me stick and I wasn't sure if I could take it from him on this occasion. I picked myself up and looked around, to see him lying on the ground behind the by-line with water being poured over him by the other England players. I felt like drowning him. It was a great goal, scored by an incredible player, but at that moment I didn't see it that way at all. When the final whistle went, all I wanted to do was get off the field as quickly as possible but I'd promised I would swap jerseys with David Seaman so I had to wait until he'd made his way down the field before I could move. And while I was standing there in the goalmouth I could see Gazza heading towards me. When he was about twenty yards away he looked at me and I looked at him and he turned away. He could see how upset I was. It was not the right time.

I had a dreadful empty feeling, which wasn't helped by the abuse coming from the terraces. Of course, that's all part of it, but on that particular day it was all too much because we had put so much into getting a result.

It was particularly bad for Gary, and there was nothing we could say to him afterwards. He sat on his own and suffered, but we all knew what he was going through. It was only when we were back in the hotel at Stratford that he felt he could talk about the penalty miss, telling us the ball had moved from the spot just as he went to take the kick. We, of course, couldn't help but kid him over that one. 'That's a good one; never heard that one before,' echoed around the room as we tried to laugh him out of his misery. But when we watched it on television that night, we saw that the ball *had* moved, and it had happened just the way Gary had said. As he took his last step forward, something happened to make the ball move that little bit. Gary's timing was affected and David Seaman saved it. Then Gazza made his way upfield to score and the dream was over. Well, almost ... because we still had a slim chance of qualifying. We had to win our game at Villa Park against the Swiss and England had to defeat Holland convincingly to enable us to go through in second place. I don't know how many of the fans really believed it could happen but we had to cling to this outside chance and, on the night, it almost happened for us. It was an unbelievable evening.

And for part of the game, that was it – we were through. We were poised to take our place among the best eight teams in Europe and then David Seaman, who had saved the penalty a few days earlier, allowed the demoralised Dutch to score at Wembley. We were suddenly back on the outside looking in, with our noses pressed to the window, unable to achieve the best finishing position that any Scotland team had ever done before.

That had been our aim from the beginning. Our objective had been to get to the quarter-finals and that was snatched away from us. As we were beating the Swiss 1-0 with a goal from Ally McCoist, England were four goals ahead of a Dutch team which had been torn apart by internal rows, but it still wasn't enough to get us through. Biased as I am, I do think we deserved to make the quarter-final stages. We had done well enough against the Dutch in the first game before their problems had surfaced and we were unlucky against England. I still feel – and I think all the lads are the same – that if that ball hadn't moved and Gary had scored, we might even have gone on to win the match. I'm certain we wouldn't have lost it. We would have been the team given a psychological boost and England would have found themselves up against it.

You have to remember the pressure England were under in that tournament, though. We certainly weren't carrying the same burden as the English lads. When it comes to these events, the Tartan Army go along hoping we will do well but not really expecting us to match up to the major players at European and World Cup level. What they want is the team to get a few decent results, to see some good performances and to be able to hold their heads high and enjoy the event for what it is – a football festival. England, though, are expected to win the World Cup again or to hold the European title, and playing at home made it even harder for them. The crowds were huge, the hype was enormous and the newspaper coverage was very often bordering on the hysterical. With a back-drop such as that, the players were expected to go out and win their games, and when they failed they found them-selves being pilloried.

I felt for Gazza, I really did – not when he scored against us at Wembley but in some of the other matches when things didn't go so well and he was left facing the blame. The critics hadn't wanted Terry Venables to play him at Euro 96, and when he did play he was the one blamed when the team was eventually knocked out. There was very little consistency about the criticisms. For my money Gascoigne remains the most gifted, skilled and influential player England have. Without him – and we have all seen this – they don't have a player who can produce a moment or two of magic to win a game. Gazza can always do that. He will either score a goal himself or create the kind of chance forwards dream about. I should know – I have watched him at close range for two years now.

Anyway, England went out to the Germans, who of course went on to win, as they have in so many other major tournaments over the years. It's never a surprise when the Germans walk off with the main prize. They've been able to do it so many times, it's almost as if their manager, whoever it may be, simply winds the players up like alarm clocks so that they go off at the right times in any competition. It scarcely ever fails. As far as I was concerned, Germany were the best team in England that summer and in Matthias Sammer they had the best player of the tournament. They always seem able to produce players who have real, solid physical strength and superb skills. I remember the first time I watched them at close range as a player, which was in Mexico. They had this full back, Pieter Brieghel, and he was massive. When we played against them in the Mexico finals he was substituted and walked off the field right in front of our bench. I could not believe the size of him. His physical presence was overwhelming. And not only do Germany always have strength; they are always the best-organised team in any of the competitions. I have great admiration for the manner in which Craig Brown prepared us for England but the Germans are always out in front of everyone else.

I still can't shake off the feeling that if Craig had only been able to get the right blend up front and got the lads up there who scored on a regular basis, then we would have been able to do even better for him. However, his defensive strategies have been magnificent. He has tried to make as few changes as possible, so the lads know each other's play, and when it's the centre three at the back of Colin Calderwood, Colin Hendry and Alan McLaren then you have players who are always ready to attack the ball and make tackles. There are few occasions when they will give the ball away in bad areas. They can all play the game and make passes when necessary, but they don't go in for silky play when it's not needed. They will only resort to that when it is appropriate and they won't take any chances around the goal – and that's how it should be. With this particular squad, it is always being said that there are no world-class performers available; that we don't have anyone to match the heroes of the past such as Jim Baxter and Denis Law. But we do have good players and over the years I think they have produced the kind of results which earlier Scotland teams were not able to do.

Gary McAllister is a class act in midfield and John Collins is not far behind him. Gary knocks the ball about in that midfield area with tremendous confidence, which can often rub off on the rest of us. The gaffer has said frequently how big an influence he has been and that's true. John Collins has taken to the continental game really well, which doesn't surprise me one little bit. Even when he was at Easter Road, before he was transferred to Celtic, John had a real passion for fitness. He was always wanting other players to go back to the ground in the afternoons and work in the gym. So he's in his element at Monaco, where all the players are of the same mind. It's good to see him have the success at Monaco – a Championship win in his first year as well as a decent run in the UEFA Cup can't be bad – because he deserves anything he earns from the game. He is one of those players who could have had a lot more caps for Scotland but for a spell he indicated that he didn't want to play in a midfield role which had him sitting out wide on the left-hand side. He always wanted to be in the middle of that area in a Paul McStay role, and when Paul and Gary were there the manager at the time, Andy Roxburgh, went with them so that John was left out. Alex Miller, our gaffer at Easter Road, used to tell him to go and play on the left and win the caps but he wouldn't listen. John has a stubborn streak in him but it's that determined edge which has helped make him such a good, good player. I can't recall too many players in the Scotland set-up in my time who have been as naturally gifted as John – yet still he works so hard to improve his game. He always wants to be that little bit better and if that means watching his diet and doing extra training then that's what he will do.

I worried about him when he was transferred to Celtic, not on the grounds of ability but simply because I thought they might push him into that position. But full marks to Celtic. They worked out a different role for him and made small alterations which gave him the scope he wanted and had not always had.

Now he is going from strength to strength. He tells us that Monaco do regular lab tests on the players, checking general well-being, fat levels and all kinds of things that British clubs don't necessarily concern themselves with. John has become a powerful advocate of this type of training and preparation and even with the Scotland squad there have been changes made in the diet of the players, especially in long-running Championships or tours when the backroom staff have you together for a fair length of time. We are not allowed any fizzy drinks, for example, and are given mineral water instead. The food is usually chicken or steak, and they keep an eye on that too, but while I can see the value of this type of thing over a sustained period of time, I don't know how effective it is during the short spells we're together with the squad.

It will come as no surprise that I am not the kind of person who goes on diets too often – not unless under a direct order from the gaffer – but I do believe in fairly sensible eating. But if something works for you, don't abandon it; what works for John might not necessarily work for me. I have to say, however, that the way John has been playing for Scotland since his move to Monaco has been fantastic.

I would like to see Duncan Ferguson getting clear of the injuries which have troubled him over the past couple of years and restricted his appearances for his country. If the big fellow had been able to play in the European Championship in England, we might have beaten England and scored more against the Swiss. The defenders in England are frightened of him and it's no wonder. He has quite awesome ability in the air, which everyone can see, and also on the ground, which too many people tend to overlook. When he came to Ibrox from Dundee United I can remember the manager stressing to the other players not just to hit long, high balls towards him because if you played it to him on the deck he could be just as dangerous. I have tremendous faith in him and I'm certain that all the potential we have seen will soon be realised. I hope he can do it at international as well as club level because that's the one area of the team where Craig has had constant problems. Players have come in and done well but there has never been that strong regular partnership which teams require if they are to score goals. Big Dunc might be able to help provide that!

The real strength, of course, has been in the off-field relationships which Craig and Alex Miller and all the others involved in the backroom have encouraged. In essence, the pool of players he has put together for Scotland is like the first-team squad at a leading club. There is a sense of togetherness and camaraderie, and that has taken us through difficult matches. Craig has managed to create that feeling which wasn't always there before. I didn't really experience the cliques which seemed to exist when I first joined the team but, as goalkeepers tend to stick together, it might not be something I would pay any attention to. Other players did complain, however, about the gap between the Anglo players and the home-based men, but that's not there now and I suppose it shows. No one in the squad is on any kind of ego trip; even the best-known players are there to do their best for the whole team rather than for themselves. That is what has helped bring us the success we have enjoyed. Sure, it's a limited success, but reaching Euro 96 and losing just one game is still better than some of the star-studded teams of the past were ever able to accomplish.

PS – When Gazza arrived back at Ibrox for pre-season training we didn't give him a chance to have a go at us. All the lads who had been with Scotland were ready when he walked into the dressing room, and we slaughtered him. He hardly had a chance to mention that England win . . .

8 Disappointments on the Continent

THERE HAVE BEEN disappointments with Rangers during my six years with the club, as well as obvious successes. Disappointment that we haven't been able to do better in the European Champions' League and disappointment that there have been times when we deserved credit for our efforts but didn't get any. But of course it is easy to take pot shots at the club and simply look at the results in the various European games without taking the trouble to look behind the results and examine the reasons why we might have failed.

I am not looking for excuses, nor am I going to offer any, but I do wish people would look a bit further than the result sometimes. There are often very obvious reasons, such as occasions when injuries have decimated the squad and the manager has been forced to play youngsters against some of the best players in the world. Then there are less visible reasons. The way the game is played in Scotland is not the way the game is played in Europe. The Premier League is a seriously competitive affair and the games can be much more intense and physical than they are in Europe. There are more 'battles' than we ever have to face in the matches on the Continent – that's just the way it's always been. Perhaps this isn't the right way, but it's certainly the way the fans want it. They want to see goals, tackles and the odd barney or two on the field. If they get that and a few nice touches here and there, then they go home relatively happy. They enjoy watching a player plough through the mud on a freezing winter's day, beat off two or three challenges from the opposition and then whack a shot into the net. Forget finesse. They just want action and the more raw and red-blooded the action, the better it is for them.

Surprisingly, there are times when Scotland try to knock the ball around the back four and the fans don't get on our backs – but try that at Ibrox and you can hear them starting to growl. They don't like it one bit and they are not long in telling you that. The last thing they want to see is the controlled, disciplined, slow build-up so beloved of the best European teams. They aren't interested in whatever we try to do – they want to see the ball sent forward into the opposition half of the field as fast as possible. So, to go back to my original point, we find ourselves having to play one way in our own League and then having to adapt our game when we go into European competitions. That brings obvious problems because switching from one style to another inside a few days is not the easiest thing for players to do.

I think the time will come when we are playing in Europe on a much more regular basis in some kind of League set-up, which would provide more games against continental opposition than we have at the moment. The chairman of Rangers, David Murray, has already talked of this possibility and as he is usually in the vanguard of moves for change it seems quite likely. It was our chairman, remember, who was among the first to talk about the Champions' League. That has been a resounding success, though bringing in the runners-up from the six most powerful countries in Europe has in some way devalued the tournament.

There is no hiding from the fact that some of our results in the 1996–97 season were poor, just as there is no hiding place whenever you take the field against some of the very best club sides in the world. Our problem, and I think English clubs have to face up to the same worries as we do in Scotland, is that playing to our strengths at home brings us success. But too often what are seen as strengths in British football become deficiencies at European level and when that happens, our teams are in serious bother. I don't think we have the opportunity to prepare for these games as well as the Europeans do. Nor do I think that these clubs have the same pressures placed on them for domestic success as we do at Rangers. If we had succeeded in Europe last year and because of that lost out on the chance of equalling the Celtic record of nine titles in a row, we would have been pilloried. Some of our most loyal supporters would never have forgiven us, and handing them a place in, say, the European Champions' League semi-final, which is where Manchester United got to last year, would not have eased their hurt. However, last season was more than a little distorted because of the record-equalling run we were attempting to put together, just as it was in 1995–96 when Celtic were trying to stop us. Incidentally, in what other country would a team go through a League programme losing just one game and still fail to take the title? That's what happened to Celtic then, and yet so many supporters inside and outside Scotland insist on telling us that winning the Scottish title is easy. It's not. It never has been. It never will be. Trying to win the League as well as being successful in Europe is another burden that is mostly carried in Britain. On the Continent most clubs will concentrate on one or the other, and somehow their fans will accept that, whereas at home the supporters want to see the Cup or the Championship even ahead of the European trophies. It goes back to that difference in attitudes which makes it so hard for us to adapt tactically from one game to the next. It would be nice to think that there would be an acceptance in the stands of the continental approach, but I just don't see it happening unless playing even more games against foreign opposition – in a League set-up, for example – would gradually educate the punters to a style of play which is welcomed in every other country in Europe but remains almost despised on this side of the Channel. When that happens we can start to look forward to a return to some success when we play these major European sides.

There are times when the general public don't seem to appreciate what we are up against as Scottish champions. We don't have automatic qualification to the Champions' League as the major powers do and that often means difficult qualifying games. Now, of course, it means *two* difficult qualifying games if you are to make it to the major part of the tournament; games which will take place before our own domestic season begins. The English clubs have never had this and while our record has been disappointing, the champions from down south have not been all that much better.

It's easy for the English fans to have a go at us but they should cast their minds back a few years to the one occasion in recent times when Rangers have met a team from south of the Border in a competitive European game. That was when we played Leeds United in the 1992–93 season, when the Champions' League was in its infancy. We had beaten the Danish champions Lyngby in the opening tie in September 1992, with goals from Mark Hateley and Pieter Huistra giving us the win at Ibrox and then Ian Durrant scoring the solitary goal of the game in Copenhagen two weeks later. It was then things became complicated. The German side Stuttgart broke the rule over foreign players in their tie with Leeds and while they won it they were forced into a Barcelona play-off with the team from Elland Road. We had been drawn to play the winners of that match and all of us, without exception, wanted Leeds to go through. Every player in the dressing room wanted to have a crack at them and to prove to the great British public that we didn't operate in some Mickey Mouse league up in Scotland. It wasn't only the Scottish players who felt that way. The English players were the same. They had played in both leagues and they knew how hard it could be in Scotland and just how much was demanded as we went for the title season after season. We felt it would be really satisfying to stuff some of the jibes back down the throats of the commentators and the fans by knocking Leeds out of the tournament and claiming a place in the last eight for ourselves.

We didn't think it would be easy, but we all thought it was possible. Having seen Leeds on the box so many times, we were all familiar with their players and style of play – unlike most European ties when you find yourselves stepping into the unknown. The gaffer and Archie Knox always watch the opposing teams so that we know the players to watch and their basic pattern of play, but with Leeds we knew so much more.

The game on 21 October 1992 was billed as 'The Battle of Britain' and 'The Match of the Decade', and it was hard to argue with those kinds of description. This was a big, big game for all of us at Ibrox as well as for the lads at Leeds. Honour was at stake – not to mention that prestigious place in the Champions' League. I honestly think that honour came before the glories of continuing in the Continent's top tournament, because this was Scotland v. England and nothing excites our supporters more than that classic confrontation.

It has been that way down through the years, and while the rivalry at international level appeared to have lessened – simply because of the demise of the British International Championship games – the old tribal enmities were there just under the surface. As we prepared for the game, we all felt that our main hope was of winning at Ibrox and then going down to Yorkshire and defending that lead because down there they would give nothing away. They were, remember, a highly rated side with extremely good players, and had even been favourably compared to the teams of the Don Revie era. They also had Howard Wilkinson, who was reputed to be one of the most tactically aware managers in the country. So when we had digested all of that, looked again at the videos and listened to Walter Smith and Archie Knox, we knew that the last thing we could afford to do was to lose a goal at Ibrox. That would hand the advantage to them and make Elland Road on 4 November an even more formidable fortress than we already believed it to be, particularly as none of our supporters were to have tickets for the return, just as Leeds fans stayed away from the first game in Glasgow. That, we believed, would work in our favour because an intimidating atmosphere at Ibrox was sure to help us.

Nothing, however, seemed to go to plan in the opening moments of that first clash. It was almost as if all our hopes, dreams and detailed planning had been tossed aside as the worst thing imaginable struck us before anyone had had time to settle . . . especially yours truly. That opening minute was one of the worst of my whole career.

They came at us from the kick-off and won a corner right away. I saw Gary McAllister standing at the edge of the penalty box and I shouted to the defence for someone to pick him up. Somehow that didn't happen. The ball dropped to him and he shot, and the ball sailed past me into the net. The worst sound in football for any goalkeeper is to hear the ball hit the net and I'll never forget how it sounded that night because the silence was incredible. The whole crowd had been stunned. I remember looking around for a linesman's flag to be raised; for anything which would mean that the strike didn't count and that we weren't a goal down so early in such a crucial game.

It was embarrassing, although I couldn't have got to the shot because Gary struck it perfectly. I can remember saying, 'Please, please go wide', but I knew that it wasn't off-target. We suddenly had a lot of hard work to do to get back into the game, but that was a season when so many of our lads were hitting peak performance at home

Brian Laudrup signs for Rangers flanked by Walter Smith and Rangers' Chairman David Murray. Goram sees Murray as one of the game's great visionaries and believes that with Murray forecasting a European League, it will surely happen.

Old Firm opponent Pat Bonner of Celtic. Far from being a deadly enemy, as a member of the goalkeeping mafia, Bonner was always willing to set traditional rivalries aside and pass on advice and tips to Goram.

Goram takes to the pitch at Wembley for Scotland's Euro '96 match with England. Colin Hendry follows with Alan Shearer in the background.

Above Manchester United Manager Alex Ferguson huddles against the cold at a training session. As part-time Manager of Scotland, it was Ferguson who first drafted Andy into the national side and took him with the squad to the World Cup finals in Mexico in 1986.

Top right The two men who have helped mould the current Scotland squad into a club-like unit. International Manager Craig Brown and his right-hand man Alex Miller. Miller was Goram's Manager at Hibs when Goram first moved to Scotland.

Bottom right Goram and his defenders work closely together. Here he discusses strategy with Colin Hendry during the clash with England at Wembley in Euro '96.

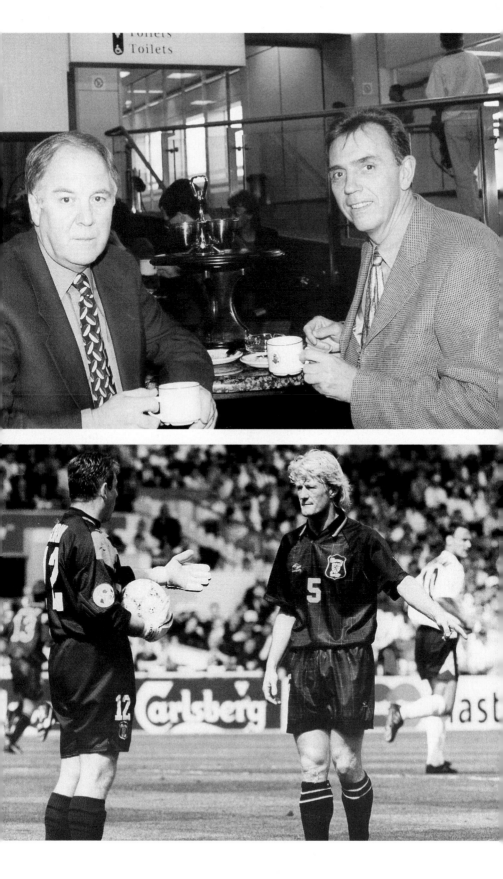

Above The best laid plans . . . The Scottish defence looks on in dismay as Alan Shearer scores England's first goal during the Wembley Euro '96 game.

Below England's second goal came from an inspired Paul Gascoigne. Gascoigne's celebration made Goram feel like punching his Rangers team mate . . .

...ove ... but sitting down and counting to ten was probably a better idea.

low The goalkeeping mafia at work. England's keeper David Seaman was quick to console ...ram after the Wembley defeat.

No consolation necessary – Goram celebrates another victory for Rangers.

and abroad. There were dodgy moments – such as that early goal we lost to Leeds – but we always seemed able to come back. There were tremendous reserves of strength, amazing determination, a refusal to acknowledge defeat and an abundance of skill. All of them were demonstrated that night at Ibrox as we shook off the shock of losing the goal and began a fight back which was to give us victory on the night and reinstate the belief that we could defeat Leeds United and march into the Champions' League to face the big guns of Europe.

After the shock of that goal from Gary we managed to get a goal in front before half-time, willed on by the huge Ibrox crowd. First of all Leeds goalkeeper John Lukic punched a corner from Ian Durrant into his own goal – a tragedy for him but a lift for us – and soon afterwards Coisty struck a second and we were in front. We stayed there for the rest of the night and, indeed, the rest of the tie.

At Elland Road on 4 November, I was in action early, and this time when the shot came in I was able to stop it. It arrived from Eric Cantona but just as he was preparing his try for goal John Brown challenged him, putting him off just a little and allowing me to save it. That helped lift the lads and when Mark Hateley scored immediately after we were on our way to that famous victory. It wasn't just that the goal from Mark gave us the cushion of a two-goal lead; it was also cancelling out any advantage Leeds might have had from the away goal in the first leg. We knew that – and they knew it too. When Ally McCoist scored a second goal for us after half-time we were through and in the Champions' League for the first time. Cantona did get the ball past me towards the end of the game but it was a token gesture of defiance from the English title holders who recognised that the tie had gone beyond their reach with Coisty's goal.

I still remember the team talk we were given by Archie Knox in the dressing room before the game. Hurling

down all the English papers on to the floor, he told us that
if being written off in the way we had been couldn't get
us going then nothing would. Our pride had been hurt.
We had been stung by the sneers from the press and
Archie and Walter knew that. But the scathing remarks
worked in our favour because so many of the lads rose to
that occasion, which turned out to be one of the biggest
in the club's history. Sure, we had some dodgy moments,
but we survived and we prospered and at the end of the
two games no one was able to downgrade our victories.
Even the English writers had to give credit where it was
due. They could scoff all they liked at the supposedly
Mickey Mouse league we were playing in but we had
beaten their champions not once but twice. And this was
the team which had won what the English call the
'strongest' league in the world.

And now the new League format awaited us, with a
draw which placed us into a group along with Marseille,
the champions of France, FC Bruges, the Belgian title
winners, and CSKA Moscow, who were the team who
had topped the Russian League table the previous season.
None of them looked too easy, but then at this level, when
just eight teams remained in Europe, what else could you
expect? This was the big time. Every team had not only
won their own titles but had since qualified for the last
eight of the tournament and there was no doubting their
pedigree. We were just happy to be in there with them. I
had suffered that disappointment against Sparta the year
before but this time we were there, right in there among
Europe's elite teams.

The draw had been kind to us in one way and awkward
in another. We started on 25 November with a home
game, which was in our favour, but we were drawn
against Marseille, the favourites to win the group and a
side who had beaten us in a pre-season friendly in Glasgow. Similarly, when the draw had been made, we had
felt good about missing AC Milan, the team everyone

tipped to win the trophy, but felt more than a little worried about the Russians, who were the dark horses in the competition having defeated the Spanish giants Barcelona en route to the final eight.

Playing the French champions proved to be one of the most incredible games of the season for several reasons. On one count we discovered that Marseille's idea of dealing with the 'physical' Scottish game was to match fire with fire. They were the hardest side we played at Ibrox all through that season, yet once again the reserves of strength and determination we were able to call on so often rescued us when it seemed that the tactics worked out by their coach, that old fox of European football, the Belgian Raymond Goethals, were going to give them victory. We were taken aback by their physical approach and before we could shake off that surprise they hit us with a goal from the Croatian striker Allen Boksic and then another from the German international Rudi Voeller ten minutes or so after half-time. There were times in that hour of play when I thought we were going to be destroyed completely. It was a terrific display from the French side but just before the end our fight back came. Substitute frontman Gary McSwegan was brought on twelve minutes from the end and within 60 seconds had scored.

Then Mark Hateley showed tremendous bravery, ducking down among the flying boots around the Marseille goal, and headed a second just a couple of minutes later. Suddenly the game was transformed, and as Goethals sent on substitute defenders, we were actually going for the winner. The French team finished the game in disarray, happy to settle for the draw. Beforehand they would have happily accepted that but after an hour's play they must have believed they were going to make a victorious start to their campaign. We had been able to avoid defeat, although we realised we had been fortunate to do so. We had to continue in the same vein. The next chance to do so was two weeks away when we played CSKA, who had been to Bruges in their first match and lost there by a single goal.

In our favour was the fact that we didn't have to face the long haul to Moscow for the game. It was out of CSKA's season and because of the climatic conditions in the Russian capital at that time of the year the European authorities had decreed that the game against us had to be played on 9 December at a neutral ground, in Bochum in Germany, a town quite close to Dusseldorf. That suited us, as did the result when the game was played.

Ian Ferguson, who had missed the game against Marseille at Ibrox, was the man who gave us victory in Germany, grabbing the only goal of the game after only quarter of an hour. It was enough to put us in second place in the group on goal difference behind Marseille, who had been able to beat Bruges by three goals in their own Velodrome.

Our placing in the section was important. It demonstrated to us how important the rescue act against Marseille had been and it kept us in touch with the French side as we moved into successive games against Bruges. The first of the two matches was in Belgium on 3 March 1993 and it was difficult because Bruges had to win after their defeat in the South of France. Anything less was going to make it impossible for them to qualify and from the manner in which they attacked us from the opening whistle it was clear that they were playing to give themselves a lifeline to the final. They probably deserved to go in front before half-time, one of their foreign players, Polish Tomasa Dzuibinski, getting their goal after 30 minutes. After that, it was almost an action replay of the last ten minutes of the opening group game at Ibrox. We were the team in command, the team who did most of the attacking, and we looked more like the home team than Bruges did. It was as if the goal had lifted us, and the support we had helped to give us fresh energy and fresh hope. The fans believed in us so much that season and we all felt that we had to give them something special to repay their loyalty. They followed us in their thousands to all the European ties – except for the one in Leeds, of course – backing us all the way and not causing the slightest bit of trouble as they did so. If they were proud of us in that campaign then we were equally as proud of them. In Germany, Belgium and France they were a credit.

We had so many chances in that third group game but their goalkeeper, a guy called Danny Verlinden, had an inspired night. There were two saves in particular which might have seen a lesser team than Rangers simply give up. He smothered a header from Dave McPherson low and just short of his line and then somehow reached a shot from Stuart McCall. It was close to the end before Pieter Huistra did get the goal we wanted, giving us a valuable point away from home. After the game, even the Belgian players admitted that the section lay between ourselves and Marseille, and we knew that to confirm that we had to defeat Bruges in front of our home support next time out. We had the added incentive that Marseille had slipped up against the Russians in Berlin, where they could only draw 1-1 with the bottom-placed side. The door remained open for us and we had to make certain it stayed that way. Only a victory over the Belgians in the return game could guarantee our qualifying for the final because even with the surprise from the other game we didn't believe that CSKA could hold out against the full might of Marseille in the second game. The Berlin result had been a shock so we could not contemplate another one. In any case, we all accepted that if we were going to qualify and get to the final of the European Cup then we would have to do so through our own efforts. This was not the kind of situation where you wanted to rely on any of the other teams. All we wanted was the chance to go in on level terms against Marseille when we met them again.

That was still within our grasp. If we both won our

next games, that was how it was going to be, and we weren't afraid of the prospect of a section decider being played at the Velodrome. There was a lot of confidence in the team as the results continued to be good on the domestic front as well as in Europe and there was a growing feeling in the dressing room that we could win the treble *and* be in the European Cup Final.

I don't think I have ever known such an exciting period in all my years at Ibrox. Going for and then getting the nine in a row was a fantastic feeling but that treble season appeared to bring just one more success after another. We were like a juggernaut as we went through game after game and still kept our dreams alive. It was quite incredible and I loved every minute of it, except for the injury I sustained against Bruges which turned out to be more serious than I thought at the time. I didn't play in any of the three games which fell between the two matches with Bruges. I rested my knee and the team played without me, Ally Maxwell, the reserve goalkeeper at the time, only losing one goal. On 17 March at Ibrox, when we did beat Bruges will always be remembered as Nissy's night because the defender scored the most spectacular goal you'll ever see. We had started the game well, playing in a very composed and comfortable style and beginning to feel fairly confident after an Ian Durrant goal – what a time Durranty had in Europe that season – had pushed us in front before half-time. Then came what could have been a disastrous refereeing decision for us.

There had been a lot of talk before the game about exactly how the Belgian side had decided to police Mark Hateley during the tie. They saw the big man as a major threat, possibly *the* major threat to their hopes, and they deployed a giant defender by the name of Rudi Cossey to take our striker out of the match. He did that, though not exactly in the way which was intended! There was a clash between the two men when Cossey seemed to try to haul Mark back by the neck. Hateley didn't like that one bit and turned to pull himself clear. The referee saw Mark do this but had missed the original foul, so called him over, showed him a red card and we were down to ten men just seconds before the half-time whistle. Suddenly, instead of being able to look forward to a second half we might have expected to control, we now had a battle on our hands. Our situation wasn't helped any when the opposition took advantage of the fact that we were down to ten men by equalising through one of their own international players, Lorenzo Staelens. It was then that Scott Nisbet stepped in with his match-saving act. He moved forward, struck a shot for goal from more than 40 yards and forced the Belgian keeper to come off his line. But the keeper had misjudged the ball, which bounced, rose high in the air and then dropped over the line as he scrambled to get back. It was incredible. Nissy has always said that he kind of tried for goal, but it hardly mattered that night. We had scored and Nissy was the hero of the night. That goal carried us into the position we wanted: level with Marseille with two group games to go. The finishing games were going to favour us because we were at home to the bottom team, CSKA, while Marseille had to go to Bruges. While the Belgians were out of the running they would still be difficult opponents on their own ground. That was how our minds were working as we realised the significance of Nissy's spectacular strike.

It was a goal which earned Nissy a special place in Ibrox folklore and the hearts of the supporters who paid him their own tribute at a testimonial when injury forced him out of the game far too early. Still, he was left with that memory above all others because it was the goal which sustained our dream for another few weeks. And as we started to think about Marseille we began to believe that we could go to their seemingly impregnable Velodrome stadium and win. In any case, we decided that we would go there and *really* try, which would place us at the top of the group and then just 90 minutes away from the final itself. It was something we had not even considered back when the campaign began, and now it was within touching distance. There was a growing sense of destiny among the players; a belief that a few more massive efforts could turn the dreams of all of us and all the fans into glorious reality. A few days before the game in France we went to Parkhead and defeated Hearts 2-1 in the Scottish Cup semi-final, keeping us in line for the treble. The final awaited but we could only concentrate on Marseille and Europe – and that's what we all intended to do. I think we felt that we had to approach the match as they had approached the first game. We had been surprised by the ferocity of their tackling and the speed of their challenges; now it was our turn and when we went out on to the Velodrome on 7 April and began to show them that we had not simply turned up as some kind of ritual sacrifice, they didn't like it at all.

They complained to the referee, the way they had played at Ibrox in the first game seemingly forgotten. They simply wanted us to roll over and let them head for the final in the Olympic Stadium in Munich. We had other ideas and as the game unfolded they realised that. Even though they scored a goal inside the first twenty minutes we refused to give way. It was their French international midfielder Franck Sauzee who scored but for us it was Durranty again who equalised soon after half-time. From that moment on they were more nervous than we were and we could sense that out there on the field. They wanted the whistle to go to end the game because they still felt that a draw, given their better goal difference, would be enough. There were moments in that second half when I really did think we were going to do it, but the game ended at 1-1 and it all hinged on the last two matches. For the first time since the tournament began we were no longer in charge of our own destiny. If both ourselves and Marseille won the last group matches then the French champions would go on to meet AC Milan.

We had to win and rely on Bruges to upset Marseille – that was the only winning route left for us. However, after the most difficult game we could have been asked to play, we still had a chance of getting to the final.

These dreams remained alive until the end of April when CSKA arrived in Glasgow. They had lost six goals against Marseille in France and were determined not to suffer a similar fate against us. They withdrew into their penalty box and camped around the eighteen yard line, making it impossible for us to break them down. We weren't helped by the fact that Mark Hateley was still missing from the team after his unfortunate red card. That had seen him banned for two games, and they were a couple of the most crucial games we were asked to play in a season which abounded in crucial games.

In this particular game, we failed to score while Marseille managed to win by a single goal in Bruges. The dream was over. At the final whistle I don't think any of us realised how close we had been and exactly what we had been able to do that season. It was only later when I sat down and considered it all that I saw we had gone through an entire European campaign without losing a single game. We had been desperately close to reaching the final and I still believe now that if we had gone there instead of Marseille then we would have beaten Milan. They did it and we could have done it too.

Maybe the thousands of fans who sat crying in the Ibrox stands that night when we knew Europe was all over thought the same. Maybe they too really believed this was the year we should have won the trophy we wanted so much. And, after it all, came the allegations against Marseille and the stripping of their European title. Bribery. Corruption. Match fixing. You name it and Marseille were found guilty of it. The Russian coach alleged that his players' food had been tampered with before they crashed to that untypical six-goal thrashing. Maybe that did happen, but I can't think of anything strange about our game there. We had taken our own food, but that's standard on most trips abroad as the club doesn't like to run the risk of any of the lads being upset by food they aren't used to. Other than Mark's sending off against Bruges, we had no complaints. We still look back on that campaign and cherish the memories.

Since these heady days, our European form has been erratic and sometimes downright embarrassing. For the next two seasons we failed to make the Champions' League, with preliminary round defeats from Levski Sofia and AEK Athens in 1993–94 and 1994–95. It's easy to say that Rangers should be able to get past that awkward opening round but the games are not easy, believe me. In fact, it is becoming more and more difficult for the champions of smaller countries – of which Scotland is one – to get to the Champions' League. Now there are two preliminary rounds and the sooner we are in a League set-up where every country has an equal chance then the better it will be. It doesn't seem right that the most powerful countries in terms of finance and the size of the television audiences they can deliver should automatically walk into the Champions' League. It isn't based on football any longer; it's based on big bucks and money talks in the corridors of power in European football and there is little Scotland or any of the other lesser nations can do about it for the moment. I do still believe that change will come and that when it does we shall become better equipped to handle the varying tactics and styles of play you find abroad, which are in such stark contrast to the way we all play football at home in the Premier League.

After the disappointments against the Bulgarians and the Greeks, we once again managed to get ourselves through to the major part of the European Cup competition. In 1995 we defeated Anorthosis of Cyprus in the preliminary round and then we followed that in 1996 with a victory over the Russian champions Alania

Vladikavkaz. But each time we went into the League set-up we seemed to shoot ourselves in the foot.

As I've said about the European Championships or the World Cup, if you get off to a bad start then you spend the rest of the time playing catch-up, which it's often not possible to do when you're playing at the highest level. In 1995, we lost our opening game in Bucharest against Steaua, old European opponents of Rangers, and then we drew at home against Borussia Dortmund a month later. Goughie and Ian Ferguson scored for us and we could justify losing a point at home because they were the German champions, and the way they performed in the tournament last season underlines how well we did against them. In December, even though Paul Gascoigne was sent off in the return, we drew with them in the second game as well, with Gordon Durie and Brian Laudrup getting the goals that night. Yet last season Manchester United, always held up as an example to us by some commentators, lost twice to virtually the same team in the semi-final of the competition. They also lost twice to Juventus, though not as badly as we did. We played the Italians in back-to-back games in the autumn of 1995 and we went into the matches without so many key players, particularly Brian Laudrup, who was out through injury. We lost 4-1 over there and then 4-0 at Ibrox and we also failed to beat the Romanians when they came to Glasgow in November. That match ended in a 1-1 draw and the Dortmund games were all we could look back on with some satisfaction. Last season was only marginally better although it began sensationally in August 1996 with our opening result against the Russians. When the draw was made none of us knew where Vladikavkaz was but we did know that Alania must be strong – any team which could be champions of such a massive country, whose national team is always one of the more powerful in World Cups and European Championships, were not going to be easy to defeat. We knew how hard it had been even against the Cypriot champions a year earlier, simply because of what is at stake for the club and the pressures that places on players. When we did discover where Vladikavkaz was we had serious doubts as to whether we would be able to reach the Champions' League. It was a long, long flight which was to take us close to the border with Chechnya, where fighting was still going on between the Chechin rebels and the Russian troops. To make matters worse, the first leg had to be played before our own domestic season had even kicked off. On paper, it seemed to be one of the most hazardous ties we could have been given. There were the travel problems, the fact we had to play them before we had kicked a competitive ball while they were halfway through their season, worries over food – over war, even – and then the actual football itself. It was, we were all sure, going to be a nightmare.

Then, as things do in football, it turned into one of the most spectacular wins in the club's many years in European football. Even the first leg did not give us any proper indication as to how it would all unravel because they played reasonably well at Ibrox, defending intelligently and hitting on the break when they could. We did win 3-1, with goals from Gordan Petric, Ally McCoist and young Derek McInnes allowing us the cushion of a two-goal lead to take with us to one of the furthermost outposts of European soccer. The away goal, though, was still a worry when we visited the Russians two weeks later.

It wasn't a worry for very long, however, because before the Russians could settle to the attacking game they wanted to play, Coisty had scored. He snapped that goal within 30 seconds of the game kicking off in Vladikavkaz and we were then off on a goal run which must have sent shock waves across the rest of the Continent. We scored seven times that day, with the other goals coming from Brian Laudrup, who helped himself to two,

Peter Van Vossen, our substitute Charlie Miller, and the
irrepressible McCoist, who completed his hat-trick. It was
a tremendous victory in a game where many had thought
we would lose and drop out of Europe almost before the
domestic season had started. The result gave us an enormous lift and perhaps that's where things began to go
wrong. Maybe we became a little too confident or maybe
we peaked too early because we had all known how vital
that first game was and how tricky it would be. To win
so overwhelmingly heightened the expectations among the
fans and the players. This time, we thought, we can repeat
the fabulous run we had enjoyed a few years earlier,
wiping out some of the disappointments we had suffered
since. Nothing is ever as simple as that, though, especially
in football. When the draw for the Champions' League
was made we were reasonably confident that we might get
through to the quarter-finals. OK, Ajax were there and we
recognised that they were Europe's form team but we did
fancy ourselves against the French champions Auxerre
and the Swiss champions Grasshoppers of Zurich. The
draw appeared to favour us too. We were asked to go to
Zurich for the first match in September and we knew that
if we could even get a draw there, we would be set up for
the second match which was at Ibrox. That was to be
against the Frenchmen and then we faced the toughest
ties: back-to-back games against Ajax with the first game
at the Amsterdam Arena. Having won and won in style
away from home in primitive conditions, we travelled to
Zurich looking for a repeat of our Russian form – although we were all too experienced to believe that we
might score another barrowload of goals. What we
wanted from the game was a decent result to set us up for
the other League games. What we got was different! We
crashed to a three-goal defeat and were never able to
match the power and skill we had demonstrated in Russia.
It was difficult to believe because Scotland had beaten
Switzerland in Euro 96 and we knew that while the

football was of a decent standard it was not so high as to worry us. Yet we lost badly and to make matters worse the Swiss players and coach criticised us afterwards. Their international striker Turkyilmaz suggested that we had arrived looking like 'holidaymakers' and this jibe was taken up back home. It was not true – we had prepared as strictly as at any other time but on the night we gave away bad goals and could not recover. It was a disastrous start to the section matches. We lost the next game 2-1 at Auxerre on 25 September, when Gazza scored for us and Richard Gough saw a shot headed off the line in the first half. If that had gone in, I believe we would have won the game and perhaps been able to turn the European season around. It's always said that there is a very thin line between success and failure in Europe and that night emphasised that for me more than any other.

Goughie's header was the turning point. By the time we reached the Ajax matches in October, we were virtually out of the running, and when we left Amsterdam we were firmly anchored at the bottom without a point to our name. I missed that game – and the return – through injury, and when Gazza was sent off early in the match our chances went with him. He knew he had let the lads down and he was inconsolable in the dressing room at half-time. He was just sitting there in tears, trying to say how sorry he was, and while Ian Durrant did get a goal late in the game we lost 4-1 on a night that Gazza and all the players really just wanted to forget. Two weeks later the roof had fallen in on us. I was still out. Gazza was suspended. Richard Gough was injured. Stuart McCall was in hospital for an operation. Alec Cleland was out. The gaffer had no option but to draft in a couple of youngsters, Scott Wilson and Greg Shields, who played particularly well in a game which Ajax won 1-0. The team still gained credit, though, for the way they matched up to the Ajax team who were virtually at full strength.

We managed one win in our half-dozen games and that

was when Grasshoppers came to Ibrox and we had a 2-1 win with both goals coming from Coisty. It gave us some satisfaction and we were able to shut up Turkyilmaz who, while we admired him as a player, had not endeared himself to any of us because of his comments on what he thought was our poor preparation for the first-leg game. The campaign ground to a halt in France at the start of December and we were out again.

Looking back, it's not easy to say exactly what went wrong – and when I do examine things I'm looking for reasons rather than trying to find excuses. There is a school of thought which says we put all our energies into qualifying; that the players realised that the Russian champions were going to be a whole lot harder to defeat than the Cypriot champions had been the year before and therefore a superhuman effort had to be made. Then, when we got to the next stage it was almost as if it was an anti-climax; that we had made our mark on Europe with the ten goals against Alania and that we expected the other games to be easier. There may be some truth in that theory. We were on a high after the Russian game and understandably so. There have been suggestions that the Russians were a poor side but these only came after we had beaten them. Beforehand everyone thought they spelled danger for us. We simply played really well over the two games and had a couple of breaks, such as Coisty scoring so early in the second-leg match. But the champions of Russia can never be dismissed.

Perhaps we did suffer from some degree of over-confidence but we did prepare as well for that game in Zurich as we did for any of the others. Another reason could be that we were consumed by the nine-in-a-row expectations of the supporters – and of ourselves, too. To some extent all the talk about that and all the hype which surrounded the League Championship and the battle between ourselves and Celtic distorted the rest of the season. Every match we played and every other tournament we took part in was overshadowed by the bid we were making to equal the record which had been held by Celtic for so long. It may seem parochial but that is how it was last year.

We had also brought in new players, just as we had in my first year with the club, and it happened over the same issue. When I arrived with several others it was because the three foreigners rule had been imposed and had bitten hard into the Rangers' squad planning. This time it was because they had scrapped the rule again – and Rangers were partly instrumental in changing things – and so they could buy players from abroad once more. What also happened, though, was that Alan McLaren and David Robertson had both had close season operations and were still missing when the programme of games began. Jorg Albertz was bought from Hamburg and Joachim Bjorklund, the Swedish defender, came in from Italy, and when we crashed that night in Zurich it was because the defence was still in the process of settling down. The problem at a club like Rangers where success is essential is that no one allows you a period where you can adjust to each other and take the odd defeat until you get things right. No, it has to be victory after victory, and while there was disappointment over Europe among the fans there was less than there would have been if we had slipped up in any of the four vital Old Firm games we had to play in the title race. We won all of them and that gave us the edge in the Championship – but that's another story.

Europe is a complicated question to address. Our basic style of play is not the one best suited to facing continental clubs and the best of the English sides have found that too. Blackburn Rovers were no better than we were when they went into the Champions' League. Manchester United did get to the semi-final but even they still lost five games in the tournament.

9 The Golden Years

SAW RECENTLY that the club chairman, David Murray, has described the years of success at Ibrox as being the 'golden years' in the history of the club. There has never been another period of sustained success as there has been over the last nine years and I just feel privileged to have been around for six of these years.

When I arrived at the club in a £1 million transfer from Hibs in the summer of 1991, I knew that Rangers were on a run of success which would be very, very difficult for any other club to halt. There was an inevitability even back then about the victories they racked up in the various competitions. And the talk at the other clubs was always about whether there was any way they could be stopped when they had so many good players and so much money. Predictably, there were constant accusations that Rangers were just 'buying the title' year after year. I didn't see it that way when I was with Hibs because I knew there had been attempts in other countries to buy success on a much more lavish scale and the teams had still failed to get the trophies they searched for. Spending loads of money was not always enough; the money had to be spent on quality players and the team had to continue winning while changes were being made to the personnel of the squad. I knew that back then but only last season was it demonstrated that money, no matter how much, will not just bring immediate success.

Poor Bryan Robson discovered that the hardest way of all at Middlesbrough when he spent more money on the team than Walter Smith has ever spent at Ibrox in one season and yet still found the club being relegated. Even appearances in two Cup Finals could not provide adequate solace for the supporters, who had believed that all the star players would make them a power in English football after spending so long away from the glare of publicity and success.

Success, then, is not directly linked to the financial resources of the club. There is more to it than that and somehow Walter Smith has been able to keep Rangers on line in a fantastic display of consistency, which is the quality above all others which brings League Championships. It is not about winning games here and there; it is about winning important games week after week after week. And then going on and doing it again the next year.

In my first season I can still recall some talk about the Celtic nine-in-a-row record of title wins, but it seemed so far away that it was only as it came closer that we began to believe that it was possible. To be honest, at the start of my Rangers career it wasn't something that I really thought was possible. It seemed incredible to think about winning nine successive Championships, especially as the competition is so fierce in every game we play in Scotland. Everyone wants to beat Rangers – every single team sees the games against us as their Cup Final – and we have to face up to that without any respite.

That has been the way in all six seasons I have been with the club and it will be the same in future years as well, although there will be less pressure this year after the ninth season of success. That brought an amazing burden on to our shoulders and while we came through, there were moments during the season when even the self-confidence we have built up in the dressing room was dented a little. People say that when you get used to the kind of pressure the Rangers players have been under down through the years, then the better equipped you are to handle it. That's true, but when other aspects intrude – when you have injuries and the weight of expectation which we had from the support last year and even the year before – then there is no doubting that something extra is being heaped on all of the players.

When I joined Rangers, it was a time when I knew that all the dreaming I had done about medals, Cup and League wins and playing in Europe on a regular basis were all going to come true. The apprenticeship was over and everything I had learned in my seasons with Oldham and then Hibs was about to help me secure a place at the very top level of club football. I did not see that as being merely at the summit in Scotland, either, because from the very beginning I saw Rangers as one of the biggest clubs in Europe. Even when you go into matches on the Continent you know from the way people speak about the club that they believe the same.

That first season was similar to what next season will be, because it found the club in a major transitional stage. The season previously, the manager who had begun the revolution at Ibrox, Graeme Souness, had left the club and gone back to be manager at Liverpool. It was then that Walter Smith was placed in charge and asked to win the Championship in the final few weeks of the season with a team which was crippled by injury. Walter did it, just as he has been doing it ever since, but it was a last-day victory over Aberdeen in May 1991 which brought the third title in succession to the club. Aberdeen had arrived in Glasgow that weekend, knowing the problems Rangers had with their team selection and surely believing they were favourites to win the game and take the title back to Pittodrie. It did not happen, of course, and so the run was underway when I arrived, along with several other players at the start of that season. The Russian captain Alexei Mikhailichenko signed, as did Stuart McCall and David Robertson, and we had to settle in quickly and help the team continue their glory run. I have said earlier how problematical that was for me at the beginning but gradually we began to gel and a lot of the credit for that goes to Richard Gough and John Brown, who were there in front of me in so many of the matches. They guided me through and we had a fantastic understanding after a couple of months or so. It's important to have that as a goalkeeper. While we lost the League Cup to Hibs, we did win the title and the Scottish Cup. It was Hearts who ran us closest for the Championship in the 1991–92 season and although they eventually finished up nine points adrift in second place, they made us work hard to clinch that one.

It was four games from the end of the season before the title was decided. When that game came round, against St Mirren on 18 April, we finished it in style with a 4-0 victory, with Coisty scoring twice and Gary Stevens and Pieter Huistra getting the others. It was a nice way to end that campaign because Saints were one of the few teams who defeated us at Ibrox that season. They had sneaked a goal in back in November and this was our revenge. Celtic and Aberdeen were the only other two teams to win at Ibrox in the League, in a season where the changes in personnel could have brought problems. In my view, it was crucial that we beat Celtic twice – both times at their ground – and drew with them once, because the haul of five points (only two points for a win back then) from the eight gave us that edge over our oldest rivals.

The next season was treble time and the best of all the years I have had with the club. 1992–93 was the year when we came so close in Europe, as well as carrying off all three domestic trophies, and I doubt if I will ever take part in a season as good as that one. I can remember Packy Bonner talking about Celtic's Centenary Year in 1988, the time they won the double, and telling me that they had about seven players that season who played to their full potential almost every week. Well, I knew what he was talking about that season because I reckon eight or nine of us would not have been able to improve too much on our performances in the games we played that year. Once again we lost just a single game to Celtic, having won two and drawn one, and while they finished third again they were well behind our total – thirteen points behind, in fact. Aberdeen were closer at nine points behind.

Once again, it was in our head-to-head games with Aberdeen that we had the advantage. We beat them three times that season and their solitary win didn't come until an end-of-season game at Pittodrie, when we had already been crowned champions. We had won it three matches earlier at Broomfield and made a little bit of history that day. It equalled the best-ever Rangers run of titles, a record which had lasted for more than 60 years, and perhaps that's when we all started to feel that if there was more history to be made then we all wanted to be a part of it. We were on a roll and we didn't want to stop. Not ever.

And yet, as is so often the case in football, just as I was thinking that way my career was interrupted by the major surgery I had to go through in Los Angeles in the summer of 1993. It was close to the end before I got back and then out I went once more. I only managed eight League appearances, the worst by far in my time with the club. It was agonising to watch as Rangers went for number six, knowing all I could do was work at trying to get back to fitness and encourage the other goalkeeper, Ally Maxwell, as much as I possibly could.

Aberdeen were back making a challenge in 1993–94 and this time it was desperately close. We edged through by only three points and we were level with the men from Pittodrie in our fourth Premier League meeting, after one win and two draws each. Celtic ended the season in fourth place as Motherwell, under their manager Tommy McLean, made their presence felt by finishing the year only a point away from Aberdeen. They had also made things harder for us by beating us twice. It was a bizarre ending to a season which saw us winning the title in Edinburgh, three games from the end of the programme.

We actually lost the game against Hibs to a goal from Keith Wright but while that was happening, Motherwell, the one team who could have caught us, lost at home themselves. They went down to Dundee United and we were champions once more, even though we lost that match and the next one against Kilmarnock before finishing the season with a disappointing goalless draw with Dundee at Ibrox. It was not the most glorious title win in the run but it counted the same as all the others did, and while I had not taken part a great deal I still felt that destiny was beckoning for the record-equalling run that the fans now perceived as being almost within touching distance. The fact that there were three seasons and more than a hundred League games to play before that could be celebrated mattered little to them. This was six and they were ready to go for it. We were carried along with them because they truly believed deep down that Rangers could equal the record and that the Celtic fans would no longer be able to boast of what their club had done in the past in the same tournament. You have to remember that a whole generation of Rangers fans grew up when Celtic were pre-eminent and their own club had not won the League for nine long years. They suffered then, just as the Celtic fans have suffered during our period of dominance, and so it had become something of a Holy Grail among them. They wanted to bring an end to the jibes they had had to suffer at the hands of Celtic fans. It was so important to them and at every Supporters' Club function we were reminded of just how important.

Inevitably, every close season brings a certain number of changes at Ibrox. That's the way football is but the summer of 1994, before we began the quest for the seventh title, the gaffer made one of his most significant

signings ever when Brian Laudrup joined the club from
Fiorentina. His contribution over the succeeding years has
been immense. I started the season but injury made itself
felt again and I played in only half the 36 games. However, I knew that I had made a contribution which was
better than the previous season and I knew, too, that this
injury was not as serious as the previous one. The
1994–95 season was the one season where Celtic got the
better of us, though it has to be said that the statistic is a
little bit artificial. They beat us in the first Old Firm game
of the season by 2-0 at Ibrox and then we defeated them
3-1 at Hampden, where they were playing their home
games that season, and after a draw (1-1) at Ibrox, they
beat us 3-0 in the last of the four games. But by then we
had taken the Championship once more and it was the
second last game of the season, and while you don't enjoy
losing to your oldest rivals at any time, it is easier to
accept when it happens in an utterly meaningless match.
Ironically, though they did do better against us that year
it did not matter one bit because they weren't the team
who were threatening us. Again, it was Motherwell, and
Hibs pushed themselves into third place with Celtic finishing fourth, eighteen points behind us. We had now moved
to the three points for a win scenario with just the one
point for a draw, though, and that's where Celtic slipped
up that season. They drew eighteen games in all.

Going back to the old system wouldn't have helped
Celtic make inroads on ourselves but they would have
done better against the two teams immediately ahead of
them in the table. They would have been level with
Motherwell, for example, and with a better goal difference would have been third.

The Championship was won five games from the end of
the season, and it was a win over Hibs at Easter Road,
with goals from Gordon Durie, Ian Durrant and Alexei
Mikhailichenko which brought the important win. After
a disappointing run of three games in March when we

drew with Hibs at Easter Road, then with Falkirk at Ibrox before losing to Hearts at Tynecastle, the lads got things together and three good results brought the title home again. They won at Tannadice against Dundee United, drew with Aberdeen at Ibrox and then celebrated the victory in Edinburgh, the same city where that Hearts defeat a month earlier had had people writing us off yet again. Over the years that has always been the best spur for the lads; to find themselves tagged as losers after all they have achieved. In times when it was suggested that the 'golden years' just might be coming to a close, there has always been a reaction from the players; a pulling together in the dressing room where on occasion harsh words have been spoken, but always for the good of the squad. We have always accepted that and when new players such as Brian Laudrup have joined the club, they have also joined in. We have been fortunate in the players the gaffer has signed, although one of them that season, Basile Boli, was an exception. He came and he went.

Boli played for most of the season but was then sold back to Marseille and finally disappeared to the Japanese League. While he was with Rangers, it was as if he never wanted to be a part of the club. He stayed apart from the other players most of the time and he never did capture the form he had shown when he played against us for the French club in the European Champions' League. Still, he was moved on and the club didn't lose money on the deal. Life went on and Boli was scarcely missed, if missed at all. It was unusual for us to have that kind of discord in the dressing room. It has been in there – in the spirit we have there – that the foundations of the club's success have been laid. If we did not get on away from the actual playing side of the game, we would lose out on a special quality which has been so important over the years. Boli did not see that, or else he chose to ignore it, and so he was soon back on the move. Walter Smith guards that dressing-room spirit as jealously as any of the players at the club. He knows how strong a motivational factor it has been and how it has helped us through any crises we may have had during the club's greatest run of success.

When the new season began in August 1995, Boli was replaced by Paul Gascoigne, who arrived to add his talents to those of Brian. We did have another player who didn't particularly want to fit in with the other players off the field. Oleg Salenko, who had starred for Russia in the World Cup finals in the United States, was bought from the Spanish club Valencia for £2.5 million. Like Boli, he didn't last long, and appeared to have the same kind of attitude. He did play fourteen full games and score seven goals but halfway through the season he had disappeared in a swap deal to the Turkish club Istanbulspor, the Dutchman Peter Van Vossen taking his place. He had not mixed, which is not an accusation you could ever level at Gazza. He fitted in straight away and in that season he played 27 League games and helped himself to fourteen goals. This time Celtic pushed us hard and even though we played well – we lost just three games in the entire season – it was the second to last match on 28 April before the eighth Championship was settled. Typically, it was Gazza who did it after we had gone a goal behind to Aberdeen at Ibrox when their defender Brian Irvine scored the first goal of the game for them. Gazza equalised for us before half-time and then scored a sensational second goal ten minutes from the end, the kind of goal which only he – and Brian Laudrup, of course – seem capable of scoring. He must have run about 70 yards, beating off half a dozen challenges before shooting, and the ball just flew past the Aberdeen keeper Michael Watt. Before the end he completed his hat-trick after Gordon Durie went down in the penalty box. The goal came courtesy of Coisty and emphasised what I have been saying about the tremendous feeling which exists in the squad of players at Ibrox. Ally had come on to the field as a substitute and there had been rumours that he might be leaving the club at the end of the season as his contract was ending that summer. He must have felt it would be nice to take the kick, because he is the main man for penalties. He has always been the guy who grabbed the ball first, ready to take the spot kicks when we got them. Ally always wants to score goals; that's what he's best at, after all, and it's what he still enjoys most about the game. Even last season, when he must have been sick of reading about how he was finished, he was the top scorer at the club when you took all games into consideration. He scored nineteen times, two more than Brian Laudrup and Paul Gascoigne. But back to that title-winning day. Gazza asked Coisty if he could take the kick and he agreed. He might have been a little bit reluctant but he let Gazza have the chance of scoring his first hat-trick for Rangers. We won the match 3-1.

While Celtic had made second place and had, incredibly, lost just one game in the entire season, they finished four points behind us. This time they had drawn eleven games and had not been able to beat us once in the whole season. There were three draws and we had the only victory of the four matches when we beat them 2-0 at Celtic Park at the beginning of the season – a psychological boost for us because a couple of weeks before we had gone to the new Celtic Park and beaten them in the quarter-final of the League Cup.

Now Celtic were left with just one more chance to stop us emulating that marvellous run they had put together in the sixties and seventies. By now our fans were moving even further ahead of themselves as they sang a new anthem from the stands: 'Eight will be great, nine will be fine but it's got to be ten in a row.' The roars emphasised – if there was any need for emphasis – just what they were demanding from us as a team. And I still think that the amount of pressure that created gave Celtic their best ever chance of winning the Championship and ending the season ahead of us over the 36 games. Again there were new faces for the 1996–97 season when we set out on the last stage of the epic journey to equal that Celtic record.

Jorg Albertz came in from the German Bundesliga team Hamburg while Joachim Bjorklund – soon to be shortened to 'Jocky' by all the players – was bought from the Italian Serie A team Vicenza, who had signed him after watching him star in Sweden's defence when they finished third in the World Cup in the United States in 1994.

There are those outside the game, and some inside the game, who talk about crucial moments in a season but in this one there were four. That's how many times we were able to win against Celtic in the League games and when the end of the season came and we had taken that ninth successive trophy, we were ahead of the Parkhead team by five points. Winning the Old Firm derby games had been the most decisive element of the season. It had never been done before since the inception of the Premier League more than twenty years earlier and all four were memorable. We won the two at Ibrox by scores of 2-0 and then 3-1 and enjoyed 1-0 victories at Parkhead – and I do mean enjoyed! No one can truly appreciate what it is like to play in these games unless they have taken part in one themselves. I always remember the gaffer telling us how even the most experienced players could suddenly go completely to pieces when an Old Firm game arrived.

For me, the second game of the season on 14 November is etched in my mind. Even now I get a shiver down my spine when I think back to the moment when the game was nearing its end and Celtic were awarded a penalty. We were in front, thanks to a goal from Brian Laudrup, and then in the second half Paul Gascoigne missed a penalty. This award for Celtic was their chance to haul themselves back on level terms and perhaps, they must have believed, stage a grandstand finish and nick the three points. Their Dutch international striker Pierre van Hooydonk, who later in the season was sold to Notts Forest, stepped forward to take the kick. And there I was, standing there in front of 50,000 supporters, knowing that everything depended on whether I could save his shot or not. That's what I mean when I say you can't adequately describe to anyone what it means to take part in an Old Firm game. It is probably the biggest test of nerve and courage that any player is asked to undergo. All I knew was that I had to save the shot – and somehow I did. Before the end we might have had a second goal when our substitute Peter Van Vossen came on to the field and managed to sky a ball high over the bar from somewhere close to the six yard box.

It was that kind of game. One dramatic moment followed another and fortunately we were able to secure another three points. When the next game loomed we were struck by a virus at the club and both Goughie and Brian Laudrup were out. Still, we were able to win and it was goals from two of the newest signings which gave us the advantage at the end. The German Jorg Albertz scored the first with a fierce free kick. When I see him strike those sort of shots I'm glad I'm playing on the same side as he is. Big Jorg has one of the most powerful shots I have ever seen and it worked well for him that day. Later Paolo Di Canio equalised and then, in the second half, Erik Bo Andersen, who had come from the Danish team Aalborg towards the end of the previous season, helped himself to a couple of goals in a quarter of an hour spell. That was victory number three.

What happened next seemed to sum up the season for us because in a sense it underlined the enormous importance which was placed on the Championship and the record we were so desperate to equal. We had to play Celtic twice inside ten days: in the Scottish Cup quarter-final on 6 March and then in the final League game. The hype surrounding the two matches was bigger than anything I had ever experienced in my entire career. These were seen as the games which were going to decide the season and after leading in the League for so long we knew that because of injuries, the jinx which has hit Rangers for so many seasons, we might be vulnerable.

Celtic, of course, were buoyed up by the fact that Gazza had been injured in the six-a-side tournament in Amsterdam and had been missing from our team ever since that Ajax-sponsored tournament in February. Also out for the Cup game was Richard Gough, and I had to take a pain-killing injection for a knock I had taken in the ribs in training. I had gone up for a cross with Gordan Petric and we had collided. It was nothing serious but it was painful and hampered my movements, so with Theo Snelders injured there was nothing for it but to take a jag and get out there. We lost goals to Malky Mackay and Di Canio and I found myself blamed for the opener. Mackay got above me but it was just one of those things and I don't think it had anything to do with the rib knock. It possibly had more to do with the absence of Goughie in front of me because over the years we developed an amazing rapport on the field. I can only remember losing a goal once through a mix-up between the two of us. It was as if there was some kind of telepathic link.

That partnership was absent again when we met Dundee United at Ibrox and we lost that game four days before we had to face Celtic once more at Parkhead in the League match. This time Richard was able to return but I was the one who missed the game, not because of the rib problem but because I was having trouble with my knee when I kicked the ball. It had flared up in training and initially I hoped that I would be able to get through the games until the end of the season and then go into hospital for a close-season operation. Just before the Old Firm game, however, the knee deteriorated a little and I knew, as did the doctor, that I would have to have the operation before the season was over. The gaffer moved quickly to make an emergency signing – Theo was still out – and Andy Dibble came up from Manchester City.

As well as that new face, the Rangers fans welcomed another more familiar 'newcomer' in striker Mark Hateley. The big man had gone to Queens Park Rangers eighteen months earlier but now, with the club in trouble because of the number of injuries, the gaffer brought him back. It was a masterstroke. Even at 35, Mark was able to terrorise the Celtic defence and it was his presence which forced their defence into a mistake which led to the solitary goal of the game, the one which gave us so much pleasure. When he rose with Celtic's latest signing from Italian football, Enrico Annoni, the ball broke from the defender and Ian Durrant took advantage to move clear down the left flank. He sent the ball into the goal and Brian Laudrup finished off the move when he forced it over the line from close range. That came before half-time and Celtic were rarely able to threaten the lads after that. Mark was sent off in the second half, as was Malky Mackay, and the game ended with our fourth win over our most deadly rivals and another little bit of history making by the team. I was just sorry that I hadn't been out there with them. I knew they were going to win; I had never seen our lads so up for anything. Even the night before the game they were buzzing in the hotel. There was this feeling that we just were not going to lose to Celtic. We wanted revenge for the Scottish Cup defeat, naturally, but we also wanted to try to make sure of the title and we wanted to do it there at Celtic Park. I had no doubts at all about the outcome of that game, even though it was another patched-up team the gaffer was forced to put out. The case was not helped when Goughie, who had trained for only a few days, had to limp off after half-time. Mind you, his job had been done by then. He had brought back stability to the defence and all the leadership qualities he had exhibited in his years at the club were on show. It was, of course, going to be his last Old Firm game and it seemed to become a personal crusade for him. He knew he had to play and he knew we had to win and his determination rubbed off on everyone in the squad.

Celtic thought that the Cup game was the vital one, possibly because they thought that they would be lifted psychologically by the victory if they got it. However, I think we all realised that the biggest prize at stake, the trophy which dominated the entire season, was the Championship. I am not suggesting for a moment that we did not want to win the cup game – you want to win all Old Firm games; you learn that very early at Ibrox – but I think we knew deep down that if we had to lose one then the Scottish Cup game could be sacrificed when the League match could not. Then, instead of giving Celtic the kind of lift they felt they would get, it worked in reverse. Our lads were stung by the two losses, to Celtic and Dundee United, and they reacted just as they have always done when things start to go wrong for them. There was a defiance about them before that final League match and a sense of purpose which had not been there before the Cup game. That, in fact, was one of the few times I sensed apprehension in the dressing room during the build-up to a game against Celtic. It was hard to put a finger on it but there was just this little feeling of nervousness, of uncertainty almost, which was entirely absent from the preparations for the return ten days later. Everything last season was altered because of the title chase. Anything we did was with winning the Championship in mind and it overrode every other consideration. It overwhelmed our thoughts at all times. If ever Celtic had an opportunity to save their record then it was last season because there were games when we stumbled towards the victories we needed to remain in front of the Parkhead team.

If you look at the statistics for that memorable season you'll find that we lost more games than we had the year before. We actually lost six matches, which was twice as many than the previous season, and we ended up seven points worse off than we had done when we fought off the Celtic challenge the year before. We lost twice to Dundee United, once at Tannadice and then at Ibrox at a critical stage of the season. We lost to Hibs and Kilmarnock and Motherwell before victory over Tommy McLean's team gave us the Championship at the second to last game of the season. Fortunately for us, when we were probably at our most vulnerable over the nine-year spell Celtic let themselves down too and we won all four of the Old Firm League games. These games, always decisive in any season as far as I'm concerned, were even more so that time round.

So many of the seasons seem to run into each other when you look back. There is a blur of games, victories and defeats. Mostly, however, what I remember is how hard it has been. It's way too easy for people, especially down south, to simply look at the nine seasons of success and say we don't have any real opposition up in Scotland. You could argue something similar about their League when you see how Alex Ferguson and his Manchester United team have dominated it for four out of the last five years. We know how hard it has been for us. When you take a close look at the various seasons then you'll find that more often than not we have gone all the way towards the closing fixtures before we have actually been able to claim the title. Nor have the winning margins been massive. The challenge has come from different clubs over the years too. Aberdeen were runners-up on five occasions, Celtic took second position twice, and Hearts and Motherwell were the others to run us close in those nine years. Before I reached the club I suppose Aberdeen were closest of all to ending the run and it required that last-day victory to ensure that it was still going on when I joined from Hibs. I can understand just how the Celtic players and their supporters must feel. In one season they lost only a single game – to us on the last day of September when we won 2-0 at Celtic Park. From then until the end of the season they didn't lose a single Premier League game and yet still could not make up the ground they needed to take away the title and stop our march towards the ninth successive win. Then, last year, when I believe we were feeling the strain more than at any other time, they were unable to take advantage of our vulnerability. The one time they were able to defeat us was in that Scottish Cup game and it must have been poor consolation for them when the season reached its end.

For us it was the end of an epic voyage and the end, too, of the squad of players whom I had joined and then served with over half a dozen of the best years of my footballing life. As I write, the chairman David Murray and manager Walter Smith are putting a fresh squad in place. Richard Gough, the most successful captain in the club's 124-year history, has gone to the United States where he has joined our former striker Mo Johnston with the Kansas City Wizards. David Robertson, who signed for Rangers around the same time as I did, has moved to Leeds United. New players from Europe have already arrived and more are set to follow. The club is entering a new era. The signing strategy follows in the wake of the Bosman ruling, which has changed the game so dramatically already, and also in the relaxation of the rules governing foreign players when clubs take part in any of the European tournaments. All of the restrictions have been swept away and as it stands Rangers will be heading into the European Champions' League or any of the other club tournaments with a side which will contain more players from Europe than from Scotland. The barriers have gone and the club is free to go for the best players they can find. The message has come from the chairman that when there are no players who are good enough within the boundaries of Scotland, then he will go into the market elsewhere. Sebastian Rozental came from Chile last season and we already had players from England, Denmark, Sweden, Germany, Australia, Holland and Yugoslavia at the club. Now they will be joined by Italian imports and the club will continue to break new ground and set the standard for other clubs in Scotland. When I moved north to Hibs, Rangers were plundering the English market. Now they have moved on and if the others, especially Celtic, don't develop as quickly and as cleverly they will be left trailing in Rangers' wake for years to come. But while the club will look towards Europe for players and for the success which has eluded them, they will always want to win the Scottish Championship. That desire will never leave Rangers.

10 The Accidental Road to Ibrox

HERE ARE TIMES in this game when you wonder just
what direction your career is going to take; times
when you know where you want to go but find it
impossible to get there until some accident gives
your life the twist it needed.

Like so many other youngsters who move to a big club
straight from school, I found myself on the scrap heap –
or what seemed to me to be the scrap heap at the time –
at West Bromwich Albion when I was still only 17 years
old. I had been one of the apprentices. Ron Atkinson had
been the manager of the Birmingham club when they
signed me but then he left to go to Manchester United and
was replaced by one-time England international Ronnie
Allen. In the shuffle which went on after his appointment,
I was released. There was no room for me at the club and
I went back to my home town Bury, wondering whether
I should try to continue my footballing career or concentrate on cricket, another sport I liked and felt I was good
at. It hurts when you're suddenly freed, especially when
you're young because you believed that a career in the
game was being mapped out for you. I wasn't helped any
when my local team, Bury, the club my father had played
for, made contact and invited me to meet the manager Jim
Iley. Down I went to Gigg Lane and was met by the
assistant manager, Wilf McGuiness, the one-time Manchester United player and manager. He told me to wait for

ten minutes or so and the manager would talk to me about the possibility of signing. I suddenly started to feel good about myself again. An hour later I walked out.

I was left sitting there for all that time and the manager didn't even bother to see me. I couldn't hack that after the West Brom disappointment, so I went home. My dad, who was upset at the way his old club had treated me, then approached Colin McDonal, Oldham's chief scout. He had been a goalkeeper himself, with Burnley, and he had been interested in taking me to Oldham before I joined up at the Hawthorns. Now he renewed that interest and this time I was signed by them as a full professional. Cricket was pushed into the background once more.

In my first season there, when Jimmy Frizzell was manager, I managed to make the first team right at the end. I played three games and thought I'd made the breakthrough I'd been looking for, much more quickly than even I had expected. However, my first-team position was soon placed on hold by the new manager, Joe Royle, a man who was to become a major influence on me. To begin with, he brought Martin Hodge from Everton on loan, and he played him, explaining to me that he needed experience in goal and that I was too young at only 18 years of age. Then Martin took ill and I was back in. While Joe kept insisting that he needed another keeper, he stuck with me and I began to convince him that even though I was young I would be able to do a job in the first team. Joe did a lot for me in my four years at Boundary Park. He brought Alan Hodgkinson into my life, who made me the goalkeeper I am today, and he brought experience into the defence in front of me. Two former Scottish international players arrived at the club – Willie Donachie and Martin Buchan – and it was amazing how much I picked up from them. In fact, I made so much progress that I was chosen for the England Under 21 team – which was followed by one of the 'accidents' which helped me get where I am today. When Gary Bailey was injured before an England match, Howard Wilkinson decided that I wasn't good enough to take over. If he *had* played me in that game, I would have been an English international and the chance of ever joining up at Ibrox would have gone. (Remember, I went to Rangers to replace Chris Woods and one of the main reasons for that was the 'three foreigners' rule which was causing the club so many problems when they played in Europe.) If Howard Wilkinson had stuck by me I would never have been able to play for the team that means so much to me now. At the time I was sick. Now I see that it was one of the luckiest things that ever happened to me. Soon afterwards there was interest from Scotland and I could play for them because my father was Scottish and, really, I was only born down south because he was playing football there. I managed to get four Scotland caps from Alex Ferguson, who was in charge of the team on a part-time basis after the death of Jock Stein, and then from Andy Roxburgh when he took over as the full-time international team boss. Fergie also took me to Mexico as the third choice keeper in the Scotland squad at the World Cup finals in 1986. And that's when transfer interest began from north of the border, only it was not from Rangers but from Hibs. Joe Royle's old club, Everton, had had a bid for me knocked back. Quite simply, they did not meet Oldham's valuation of me, which was something more than £300,000. Hibs then stepped in with an acceptable offer and I signed for them in October 1987.

It was strange that I should be going to Scotland and back to my father's old club; he had played at Easter Road before moving south to Bury. I had heard some whispers that Rangers might be interested and I had spent time with their manager Graeme Souness and his right-hand man Walter Smith in Mexico when Graeme was captain and Walter assistant manager. Nothing happened, though, and nothing did happen for several more years, but I felt that the move to Hibs was right for me. I decided that playing in Scotland might help my international chances, a definite factor in making the move to Edinburgh.

There was a bit of pressure on me right from the start because I was Hibs' biggest ever signing – and that isn't often a tag you can attach to a goalkeeper. My old mate Alan Rough, who had been with Scotland, was the first choice keeper until I arrived. It wasn't easy for him when he went out but he was always great to me and, while his approach to keeping goal was a whole lot different to anyone else's I learned a lot from him. He was so laid back he was almost horizontal. Nothing ever seemed to worry him.

I had some really good times at Hibs. I went into Europe for the first time with them in the UEFA Cup in the 1989–90 season and eventually the manager, Alex Miller, who is now with Coventry as well as being a vital member of Scotland manager Craig Brown's backroom staff, made me the team captain. Very importantly, I felt that I was learning more and more about my chosen trade. I was performing at a higher level than I had with Oldham because while I was there the team remained in the old Second Division. While I had been capped while playing in one of the lower Leagues, you do worry about that situation. There is always the nagging worry at the back of your mind that someone playing in one of the top divisions will be preferred to you when the international call comes. So the transfer to Hibs and the time I spent at Easter Road were of tremendous benefit to me and I like to think that I gave them value for money too. I think Alex Miller believed that I did. We had our disagreements, of course, which is only natural because I have never been one who buckles down easily to discipline. There was one particular headline incident when I defied him and went to play cricket for Scotland against the Australians while Hibs were involved in pre-season training. It was wrong of me and I was fined substantially by the club, but when the opportunity arose I just couldn't refuse. I was warned beforehand that I would be fined so I had no complaints when it happened. When I went to Rangers, though, I knew my cricketing days were over. The gaffer just told me straight when I signed that cricket was out. He wasn't paying a million pounds, he told me, for a goalie who might break a finger playing cricket and then be sidelined for important games. That time I didn't argue, because the move to Rangers was the one I had really wanted. Joining Hibs and playing for them in a couple of European games had taken me one step up the ladder, whetting my appetite for more big-time matches. Now the next step had to be taken and I felt I was ready for it. If I *had* been given the chance of joining Rangers from Oldham it would have been too soon, although at the time I was confident that I would be able to handle it. All the brashness of youth – something I was not short on then – made me believe that I was good enough to play for any team anywhere. But I wasn't. I needed the time at Hibs just as I had needed that four-year learning spell at Oldham. What I had in abundance was natural ability, a good eye and good co-ordination, but it was Hodgy's tuition and the experience of the Scottish Premier League which made me a good enough keeper to play for Rangers.

I'm not one of those who knock the Premier League set-up. I know there are players who don't like it; who find playing each other four times a season too much. My old Hibs mate John Collins left Celtic to go to Monaco, and that 'sameness' of the game in Scotland influenced his decision. David Robertson went to Leeds at the end of last season, he too complaining of 'staleness'. Maybe I don't feel it the same as an outfield player does but I can never think of any occasion when I have felt that way. I enjoy the games and the challenges which are thrown up by other clubs as much now as I did when I first began to play in the Top Ten. I don't see any real need to change it. The biggest clubs in Scotland are in the League and that's what matters. The level of competition is high and we never forget that at Rangers. While we keep on winning titles, it doesn't get any easier as the years go by. Not only are there good players in Scotland; there is effective organisation and a determination, so much a part of the Scottish game, which present even the best of teams with problems. Determination is a quality which has helped the nation at international level and it's something you can't ever ignore.

You underestimate teams at your peril – and that is something which keeps me on my toes. Scottish football is exciting, and there's never any shortage of action. The contest between ourselves and Celtic, especially over the past couple of years, has been gripping. You have only to look at the crowds that have been attracted to both Ibrox and Celtic Park in that period. Both clubs have around 40,000 season ticket holders and the average attendances are way up around 50,000 per game. Not too many cities can boast that level of interest so there can't be too much wrong with the domestic game.

Last season did carry a lot of strain but the 'nine in a row' business is over now, and while the target has become ten I don't think the Championship will dominate the season as much as it did last time round. In all honesty, I hope it doesn't, because there was a sense of unreality at times last year and the pressure on the players and the managers at both clubs was immense. Still, that is part and parcel of being a Rangers player. This is a club and a support which has been reared on success. There have been lean years but Rangers have constantly striven to be the top team in Scotland and one of the major clubs in Britain and even Europe. I am proud that I have been a part of this Ibrox revolution.

I missed the initial years when Graeme Souness changed the face of Scottish football for ever, but in my time there have been changes and now the chairman David Murray and the manager have embarked on another strategy. The exciting thing about being at Ibrox is that there will always be change; that the club will never be content to stand still; that no matter what success they might achieve, they will always be searching for more fields to conquer. Every close season the club has been able to offer the supporters new players and fresh excitement and in these rapidly changing times in the game I'm sure they will continue with that policy. Perhaps one day the success in the Premier League will end but I don't see it happening in the foreseeable future. Rangers simply seem to be getting stronger and stronger and the more we win the more we want to win. No one is allowed to rest on their laurels at Rangers. From the chairman down through the manager to the backroom staff and to the players, everyone is expected to perform at their highest level all the time.

I have made mistakes in my time, as you will know having read this book. I like to have a drink and I like to play the horses. But I still believe that you can work hard and play hard, and that's something which has been a binding force among the players at Ibrox. There may have been mistakes but there is not a lot I regret because these have been the very best of times.

STATISTICS
1991–1997

```
┌─────────────────────────────────────────┐
│              GRID KEY                    │
│                                          │
│  PL: Premier League    Skol: Skol Cup    │
│  EC: European Cup      CC: Coca Cola Cup │
│  SC: Scottish Cup      F: Friendly       │
│                        LC: League Cup    │
└─────────────────────────────────────────┘
```

Andy Goram

Results 1991–92

DATE	OPPOSITION	VENUE	COMP	SCORE	CROWD	1	2	3
Aug 10	St Johnstone	H	PL	6-0	35,109	Goram	Stevens	D. Roberts
Aug 13	Motherwell	H	PL	2-0	35,322	Goram	Stevens	D. Roberts
Aug 17	Hearts	A	PL	0-1	22,154	Goram	Stevens	D. Roberts
Aug 20	Queen's Park	H	Skol	6-0	32,230	Goram	Stevens	D. Roberts
Aug 24	Dunfermline	H	PL	4-0	35,559	Goram	Stevens	D. Roberts
Aug 28	Partick Thistle	A	Skol	2-0	12,587	Goram	Stevens	D. Roberts
Aug 31	Celtic	A	PL	2-0	51,381	Goram	Stevens	D. Roberts
Sep 4	Hearts	A	Skol	1-0	22,878	Goram	Stevens	D. Roberts
Sep 7	Falkirk	A	PL	2-0	13,088	Goram	Stevens	D. Roberts
Sep 14	Dundee United	H	PL	1-1	36,347	Goram	Stevens	D. Roberts
Sep 18	Sparta Prague	A	EC	0-1	11,053	Goram	Stevens	D. Roberts
Sep 21	St Mirren	A	PL	2-1	14,438	Goram	Stevens	D. Roberts
Sep 25	Hibernian	Hamp	Skol	0-1	40,901	Goram	Stevens	D. Roberts
Sep 28	Aberdeen	H	PL	0-2	36,330	Goram	Stevens	D. Roberts
Oct 2	Sparta Prague	H	EC	2-1	34,260	Goram	Stevens	D. Roberts

After extra-time: score after 90 minutes 0-0. Aggregate score 2-2. Sparta Prague win on away goals.

DATE	OPPOSITION	VENUE	COMP	SCORE	CROWD	1	2	3
Oct 5	Airdrie	A	PL	4-0	10,200	Goram	Stevens	D. Roberts
Oct 8	Hibernian	H	PL	4-2	35,368	Goram	Stevens	D. Roberts
Oct 12	St Johnstone	A	PL	3-2	10,323	Goram	Stevens	D. Roberts
Oct 19	Hearts	H	PL	2-0	36,481	Goram	Stevens	D. Roberts
Oct 26	Falkirk	H	PL	1-1	36,441	Goram	Stevens	D. Roberts
Oct 29	Dundee United	A	PL	2-3	14,397	Goram	Stevens	D. Roberts
Nov 2	Celtic	H	PL	1-1	37,387	Goram	Stevens	D. Roberts
Nov 9	Dunfermline	A	PL	5-0	13,351	Goram	Stevens	D. Roberts
Nov 16	Airdrie	H	PL	4-0	36,934	Goram	Stevens	D. Roberts
Nov 19	Hibernian	A	PL	3-0	16,653	Goram	Stevens	D. Roberts
Nov 23	St Mirren	H	PL	0-1	36,272	Goram	Stevens	D. Roberts
Nov 30	Motherwell	A	PL	2-0	15,350	Goram	Stevens	D. Roberts
Dec 4	Aberdeen	A	PL	3-2	22,000	Goram	Stevens	D. Roberts
Dec 7	St Johnstone	H	PL	3-1	35,784	Goram	Stevens	D. Roberts
Dec 14	Falkirk	A	PL	3-1	12,000	Goram	Stevens	D. Roberts
Dec 21	Dundee United	H	PL	2-0	41,448	Goram	Stevens	D. Roberts
Dec 28	Dunfermline	H	PL	2-1	41,328	Goram	Stevens	D. Roberts
Jan 1	Celtic	A	PL	3-1	50,802	Goram	Stevens	D. Roberts
Jan 4	Airdrie	A	PL	0-0	10,209	Goram	Stevens	D. Roberts
Jan 11	Hibernian	H	PL	2-0	40,616	Goram	Stevens	D. Roberts
Jan 18	Motherwell	H	PL	2-0	38,217	Goram	Stevens	D. Roberts
Jan 22	Aberdeen	A	SC	1-0	22,000	Goram	Stevens	D. Roberts
Feb 1	Hearts	A	PL	1-0	24,356	Goram	Stevens	D. Roberts
Feb 8	St Mirren	A	PL	2-1	16,638	Goram	Stevens	D. Roberts
Feb 15	Motherwell	H	SC	2-1	38,444	Goram	Stevens	D. Roberts
Feb 25	Aberdeen	A	PL	0-0	38,518	Goram	Stevens	D. Roberts
Feb 29	Airdrie	H	PL	5-0	40,568	Goram	Stevens	D. Roberts
Mar 3	St Johnstone	A	SC	3-0	10,107	Goram	Stevens	D. Roberts
Mar 10	Hibernian	A	PL	3-0	13,019	Goram	Stevens	D. Roberts
Mar 14	Dunfermline	A	PL	3-0	12,274	Goram	Stevens	D. Roberts
Mar 21	Celtic	H	PL	0-2	42,160	Goram	Stevens	D. Roberts
Mar 28	St Johnstone	A	PL	2-1	9,697	Goram	Stevens	D. Roberts
Mar 31	Celtic	Hamp	SC	1-0	45,191	Goram	Stevens	D. Roberts
Apr 7	Falkirk	H	PL	4-1	36,382	Goram	Stevens	Kuznetso
Apr 11	Dundee United	A	PL	2-1	11,391	Goram	Stevens	D. Roberts
Apr 18	St Mirren	H	PL	4-0	40,362	Goram	Stevens	Vinnicom

4	5	6	7	8	9	10	11
Gough	Spackman	Nisbet	Steven	Ferguson	Hateley 3	Johnston 2	Huistra
Gough	Spackman	Nisbet	Steven	Ferguson	Hateley	Johnston	Huistra
Gough	Spackman	Nisbet	McCall	Ferguson	Hateley	Johnston	Huistra
Gough	Spackman	Nisbet	McCall	Johnston 4	Spencer	Durrant	Huistra
Gough	Spackman	Nisbet	McCall	Spencer	Johnston	Durrant	Huistra
Gough	Spackman	Nisbet	McCall	Spencer	Johnston	Durrant	Huistra
Gough	Spackman	Nisbet	McCall	Ferguson	Hateley 2	Johnston	Huistra
Gough	Spackman	Nisbet	McCall	Ferguson	Hateley	Johnston	McCoist
Gough	Spackman	Nisbet	McCoist	Ferguson	Hateley	Mik'chenko	Huistra
Kuznetsov	Spackman	Nisbet	McCoist	Ferguson	Hateley	Mik'chenko	Huistra
Gough	Spackman	Nisbet	McCall	Ferguson	Hateley	McCoist	Huistra
Other substitutes: McKellar, S. Robertson, Spencer							
Gough	Spackman	Nisbet	McCall	Durrant	Hateley	Johnston	Huistra
Brown	Spackman	Nisbet	McCall	Durrant	Hateley	Johnston	Huistra
Brown	Spackman	Nisbet	McCall	S. Robertson	Hateley	Johnston	Mik'chenko
Brown	Spackman	Nisbet	Kuznetsov	McCall 2	McCoist	Johnston	Mik'chenko
Other substitutes: McKellar, S. Robertson, McSwegan							
Kuznetsov	Spackman	Nisbet	Mik'chenko	McCall	McCoist 2	Johnston	Huistra
Brown	Spackman	Nisbet	S. Robertson	McCall	McCoist 2	Johnston	Huistra
McGregor	Spackman	Nisbet	Morrow	McCall	McCoist 2	Durrant	Spencer
Gough	Spackman	Nisbet	Morrow	McCall	McCoist	Hateley	Mik'chenko
Gough	Spackman	Nisbet	Morrow	McCall	McCoist	Johnston	Mik'chenko
Brown	Spackman	Nisbet	Ferguson	McCall	McCoist 2	Hateley	Huistra
Gough	Spackman	Nisbet	McCall	Ferguson	McCoist	Hateley	Huistra
Gough	Spackman	Nisbet	Gordon 2	McCall	McCoist	Hateley	Huistra
Gough	Spackman	Kuznetsov	Gordon	McCall	McCoist	Hateley 2	Huistra
Gough	Spackman	Kuznetsov	Gordon	McCall	McCoist 2	Hateley	Huistra
Gough	Spackman	Kuznetsov	Gordon	McCall	McCoist	Hateley	Huistra
Gough	Spackman	Kuznetsov	Gordon	McCall	McCoist	Hateley	Mik'chenko
Gough	Spackman	Kuznetsov	Gordon	McCall	McCoist	Hateley 2	Mik'chenko
Gough	Spackman	Kuznetsov	Gordon	McCall	McCoist	Hateley	Mik'chenko
Gough	Spackman	Kuznetsov	Gordon	McCall	McCoist	Hateley	Mik'chenko
Gough	Spackman	Kuznetsov	Gordon	McCall	McCoist 2	Hateley	Mik'chenko
Gough	Ferguson	Kuznetsov	Gordon	McCall	McCoist	Spencer	Mik'chenko
Gough	Spackman	Kuznetsov	Gordon	McCall	McCoist	Hateley	Mik'chenko
Gough	Spackman	Kuznetsov	Gordon	Brown	McCoist	Huistra	Mik'chenko
Gough	Spackman	Brown	Gordon	McCall	McCoist	Rideout	Mik'chenko
Gough	Spackman	Brown	Gordon	McCall	McCoist	Rideout	Mik'chenko
Gough	Spackman	Brown	Gordon	McCall	McCoist	Ferguson	Mik'chenko
Gough	Spackman	Brown	Gordon	McCall	McCoist	Rideout	Mik'chenko
Gough	Spackman	Brown	Gordon	McCall	McCoist	Rideout	Mik'chenko
Gough	Spackman	Brown	Gordon	Ferguson	McCoist	Rideout	Mik'chenko 2
Gough	Spackman	Brown	Gordon	Ferguson	McCoist	Hateley	Huistra
Gough	Spackman	Brown	Gordon	Ferguson	McCoist	Hateley 3	Huistra
Gough	Spackman	Brown	Gordon	Ferguson	McCoist	Hateley	Huistra
Nisbet	Spackman	Brown	Gordon	McCall	McCoist	Hateley 2	Huistra
Nisbet	Spackman	Brown	Mik'chenko 2	McCall	McCoist	Hateley	Huistra
Nisbet	Spackman	Brown	Ferguson	McCall	McCoist	Hateley	Mik'chenko
Gough	Spackman	Brown	Spencer	Durrant	McCoist	Hateley 2	Huistra
Gough	Spackman	Brown	Gordon	McCall	McCoist	Durrant	Huistra
Gough	Spackman	Brown	Gordon	McCall	McCoist 3	Durrant	Huistra
Gough	Spackman	Brown	Gordon	McCall	McCoist	Durrant	Mik'chenko
Gough	Spackman	Brown	Gordon	McCall	McCoist 2	Durrant	Mik'chenko

Results 1991–92 *Continued*

DATE	OPPOSITION	VENUE	COMP	SCORE	CROWD	1	2	3
Apr 23	Motherwell	A	PL	2-1	12,515	Goram	Stevens	D. Robertson
Apr 28	Hearts	H	PL	1-1	36,129	Goram	Kuznetsov	D. Robertson
May 2	Aberdeen	A	PL	2-0	17,000	Goram	Stevens	D. Robertson
May 9	Airdrie	Hamp	SC	2-1	44,045	Goram	Stevens	D. Robertson

4	5	6	7	8	9	10	11
Kuznetsov	Spackman	Rideout	Huistra	S. Robertson	McCoist	Durrant	Mik'chenko 2
Rideout	Spackman	Brown	L. Robertson	McCall	McCoist	Hateley	Huistra
Gough	Rideout	Durrant	Gordon	McCall	McCoist 2	Hateley	Mik'chenko
Gough	Spackman	Brown	Durrant	McCall	McCoist	Hateley	Mik'chenko

Results 1992–93

DATE	OPPOSITION	VENUE	COMP	SCORE	CROWD	1	2	3
Aug 1	St Johnstone	H	PL	1-0	38,036	Goram	Nisbet	D. Roberts
Aug 4	Airdrie	H	PL	2-0	34,613	Goram	Nisbet	D. Roberts
Aug 8	Hibernian	A	PL	0-0	17,044	Goram	Nisbet	D. Roberts
Aug 11	Dumbarton	Hamp	Skol	5-0	11,091	Maxwell	Nisbet	D. Roberts
Aug 15	Dundee	A	PL	3-4	12,807	Maxwell	Nisbet	D. Roberts
Aug 19	Stranraer	A	Skol	5-0	4,500	Goram	Murray	D. Roberts
Aug 22	Celtic	H	PL	1-1	43,239	Goram	Ferguson	D. Roberts
Aug 26	Dundee United	A	Skol	3-2	15,716	Goram	Spackman	D. Roberts
Aug 29	Aberdeen	H	PL	3-1	41,636	Goram	Spackman	D. Roberts
Sep 2	Motherwell	A	PL	4-1	10,074	Goram	Spackman	D. Roberts
Sep 12	Partick Thistle	A	PL	4-1	10,460	Goram	McCall	D. Roberts
Sep 16	Lyngby	H	EC	2-0	40,036	Goram	Durrant	D. Roberts
Sep 19	Hearts	H	PL	2-0	41,888	Goram	McCall	D. Roberts
Sep 22	St Johnstone	Hamp	Skol	3-1	30,062	Goram	McCall	D. Roberts
Sep 26	Dundee United	A	PL	4-0	13,515	Goram	McCall	D. Roberts
Sep 30	Lyngby	A	EC	1-0	4,273	Goram	McCall	D. Roberts
Oct 3	Falkirk	H	PL	4-0	40,691	Goram	Nisbet	D. Roberts
Oct 7	St Johnstone	A	PL	5-1	9,532	Goram	Nisbet	D. Roberts
Oct 17	Hibernian	H	PL	1-0	40,978	Goram	Kuznetsov	D. Roberts
Oct 21	Leeds United	H	EC	2-1	43,251	Goram	McCall	D. Roberts
Oct 25	Aberdeen	Hamp	Skol	2-1	45,298	Goram	McCall	D. Roberts
Oct 31	Motherwell	H	PL	4-2	38,719	Goram	Kuznetsov	D. Roberts
Nov 4	Leeds United	A	EC	2-1	25,118	Goram	McCall	D. Roberts
Nov 7	Celtic	A	PL	1-0	51,958	Goram	McCall	D. Roberts
Nov 11	Dundee	H	PL	3-1	33,497	Goram	Stevens	D. Roberts
Nov 21	Hearts	A	PL	1-1	20,831	Goram	Stevens	D. Roberts
Nov 25	Marseille	H	EC	2-2	41,624	Goram	Murray	D. Roberts
Nov 28	Partick Thistle	H	PL	3-0	40,939	Goram	Stevens	D. Roberts
Dec 1	Airdrie	A	PL	1-1	8,000	Goram	Stevens	D. Roberts
Dec 9	CSKA Moscow	A	EC	1-0	9,000	Goram	McCall	D. Roberts
Dec 12	Falkirk	A	PL	2-1	12,000	Goram	Pressley	D. Roberts
Dec 19	St Johnstone	H	PL	2-0	35,369	Goram	Pressley	D. Roberts
Dec 26	Dundee	A	PL	3-1	13,983	Goram	Pressley	D. Roberts
Jan 2	Celtic	H	PL	1-0	46,039	Goram	McCall	D. Roberts
Jan 5	Dundee United	H	PL	3-2	40,239	Goram	McCall	D. Roberts
Jan 9	Motherwell	A	SC	2-0	14,314	Goram	Nisbet	D. Roberts
Jan 30	Hibernian	A	PL	4-3	17,444	Goram	Stevens	D. Roberts
Feb 2	Aberdeen	A	PL	1-0	15,500	Goram	Stevens	D. Roberts
Feb 6	Ayr United	A	SC	2-0	13,176	Goram	Stevens	D. Roberts
Feb 9	Falkirk	H	PL	5-0	34,780	Goram	Stevens	D. Roberts
Feb 13	Airdrie	H	PL	2-2	39,816	Goram	Stevens	D. Roberts
Feb 20	Dundee United	A	PL	0-0	13,234	Goram	Stevens	D. Roberts
Feb 23	Motherwell	A	PL	4-0	14,006	Goram	McCall	D. Roberts
Feb 27	Hearts	H	PL	2-1	42,128	Goram	Nisbet	D. Roberts
Mar 3	Bruges	A	EC	1-1	19,000	Goram	Nisbet	D. Roberts
Mar 6	Arbroath	A	SC	3-0	6,488	Maxwell	Nisbet	D. Roberts

4	5	6	7	8	9	10	11
Gough	McPherson	Brown	Durrant	McCall	McCoist	Hateley	Huistra
Gough	Kuznetsov	Brown	Gordon	McCall	McCoist	Hateley	Mik'chenko
Gough	McPherson	Brown	Steven	McCall	McCoist	Hateley	Gordon
Gough	McPherson	Durrant	Gordon	McCall	McCoist	Hateley	Mik'chenko
Gough	McPherson	Brown	Gordon	McCall	McCoist 2	Hateley	Mik'chenko
Gough	McPherson	Ferguson	Durrant	McCall	McCoist 3	Hateley 2	Huistra
Gough	McPherson	Brown	Steven	McCall	McCoist	Hateley	Huistra
Gough	McPherson	Brown	Durrant	Ferguson	McCoist	McSwegan	Huistra
Gough	McPherson	Brown	Durrant	Ferguson	McCoist	Mik'chenko	Huistra
Gough	McPherson	Brown	Durrant	Ferguson	McCoist 3	Mik'chenko	Huistra
Gough	McPherson	Brown	Huistra	Ferguson	McCoist	Durrant	Mik'chenko
Gough	McPherson	Brown	Mik'chenko	Ferguson	McCoist	Hateley	Huistra
Other substitutes: Maxwell, S. Robertson, Hagen							
Gough	McPherson	Brown	Steven	Ferguson	McCoist	Durrant	Huistra
Gough	McPherson	Brown	Durrant	Ferguson	McCoist 3	Hateley	Huistra
Gordon	Nisbet	Brown	Steven	Ferguson	McCoist	Hateley	Huistra 2
Durrant	McPherson	Brown	Steven	Ferguson	McCoist	Hateley	Huistra
Other substitutes: Maxwell, Murray, McSwegan. Rangers win 3-0 on aggregate							
Gordon	McPherson	Brown	McCall	Ferguson	McCoist 4	Hateley	Huistra
McCall	McPherson	Durrant	Steven	Ferguson	McCoist 2	Hateley 2	Huistra
Gough	Mik'chenko	Brown	Steven	Ferguson	Durrant	Hateley	Huistra
Gough	McPherson	Brown	Steven	Ferguson	McCoist	Hateley	Durrant
Other substitutes: Maxwell, Murray, McSwegan							
Gough	McPherson	Brown	Steven	Ferguson	McCoist	Hateley	Durrant
Gordon	McPherson	Brown	McCall	Ferguson	McCoist 3	Mik'chenko	Huistra
Gough	McPherson	Brown	Gordon	Ferguson	McCoist	Hateley	Durrant
Other substitutes: Maxwell, Murray, McSwegan. Rangers win 4-2 on aggregate							
Gough	McPherson	Brown	Gordon	Ferguson	McCoist	Hateley	Durrant
Durrant	McPherson	Brown	McCall	Ferguson	McCoist 2	Hateley	Huistra
Gordon	McPherson	Brown	Steven	Ferguson	McCoist	Hateley	Huistra
Gough	McPherson	Brown	Steven	McCall	Durrant	Hateley	Mik'chenko
Other substitutes: Maxwell, Hagen, Dodd							
Gordon	McPherson	Brown	Steven	Ferguson	McSwegan	McCall	Huistra
Durrant	Pressley	Brown	Steven	Ferguson	McSwegan	Hateley	Mik'chenko
Durrant	McPherson	Brown	Steven	Ferguson	McCoist	Hateley	Mik'chenko
Other substitutes: Maxwell, Pressley, Hagen							
Durrant	McPherson	Brown	Gordon	McCall	McCoist	Hateley	Mik'chenko
Gough	McPherson	Durrant	Steven	McCall	McCoist	Hateley	Huistra
Gough	McPherson	McCall	Steven	Ferguson	McCoist	Hateley 2	Durrant
Gough	McPherson	Brown	Steven	Ferguson	Gordon	Hateley	Durrant
Gough	McPherson	Brown	Steven	Ferguson	McCoist	Hateley	Mik'chenko
Gordon	McPherson	Brown	Steven	McCall	McCoist 2	Hateley	Mik'chenko
Gordon	McPherson	Brown	Steven	McCall	McCoist	Hateley 2	Mik'chenko
Gordon	McPherson	Brown	Steven	McCall	McCoist	Hateley	Mik'chenko
Gordon	Nisbet	Brown	Steven	McCall	McCoist	Hateley	Mik'chenko
Gough	Kuznetsov	Brown	Steven	McCall	McCoist	Hateley 2	Huistra
Gough	Kuznetsov	Brown	Steven	Mik'chenko	McCoist 2	Hateley	Huistra
Gough	McPherson	Murray	McCall	Ferguson	McCoist	Hateley	Huistra
Gough	McPherson	Brown	Steven	Ferguson	McCoist	Hateley 2	Huistra
McCall	McPherson	Brown	Gordon	Ferguson	McCoist	Hateley	Huistra
Murray	McPherson	Brown	Mik'chenko	McCall	McCoist	Hateley	Huistra
Other substitutes: Maxwell, McSwegan, Hagen							
Murray	McPherson	Brown	Mik'chenko	McCall	McCoist	Hateley	Huistra

Results 1992–93 *Continued*

DATE	OPPOSITION	VENUE	COMP	SCORE	CROWD	1	2	3
Mar 10	St Johnstone	A	PL	1-1	9,210	Maxwell	Nisbet	D. Robertson
Mar 13	Hibernian	H	PL	3-0	41,076	Maxwell	McCall	D. Robertson
Mar 17	Bruges	H	EC	2-1	42,731	Goram	Nisbet	Murray
Mar 20	Celtic	A	PL	1-2	53,241	Goram	Nisbet	D. Robertson
Mar 27	Dundee	H	PL	3-0	40,294	Maxwell	McCall	D. Robertson
Mar 30	Aberdeen	H	PL	2-0	44,570	Goram	McCall	D. Robertson
Apr 3	Hearts	Pkhd	SC	2-1	41,738	Goram	McCall	D. Robertson
Apr 7	Marseille	A	EC	1-1	40,000	Goram	McCall	D. Robertson
Apr 10	Motherwell	H	PL	1-0	41,353	Maxwell	McCall	Murray
Apr 14	Hearts	A	PL	3-2	14,622	Maxwell	McCall	Watson
Apr 17	Partick Thistle	H	PL	3-1	42,636	Maxwell	McCall	Watson
Apr 21	CSKA Moscow	H	EC	0-0	43,142	Goram	McCall	D. Robertson
May 1	Airdrie	A	PL	1-0	11,830	Goram	McCall	D. Robertson
May 4	Partick Thistle	A	PL	0-3	9,834	Maxwell	Murray	Watson
May 8	Dundee United	H	PL			Maxwell	Kuznetsov	D. Robertson
May 12	Aberdeen	A	PL			Maxwell	Murray	Kuznetsov
May 15	Falkirk	A	PL			Maxwell	Murray	D. Robertson
May 29	Aberdeen	Pkhd	SC			Goram	McPherson	D. Robertson

4	5	6	7	8	9	10	11
Murray	McPherson	Brown	Steven	McCall	McCoist	Hateley	Mik'chenko
Murray	McPherson	Brown	Pressley	Durrant	McCoist	Hateley	Hagen
Gough	McPherson	Brown	Steven	McCall	McCoist	Hateley	Durrant
Other substitutes: Maxwell, Pressley, McSwegan							
Murray	McPherson	Brown	Steven	Hagen	McCall	Hateley	Durrant
Gough	McPherson	Brown	Steven	Ferguson	McCoist	Hateley	Huistra
Gough	McPherson	Brown	Steven	Ferguson	McCoist	Hateley	Huistra
Gough	McPherson	Brown	Steven	Ferguson	McCoist	Hateley	Hagen
Gough	McPherson	Brown	Steven	Ferguson	McCoist	Durrant	Huistra
Other substitutes: Maxwell, Pressley, Kuznetsov							
Gough	McPherson	Brown	Steven	Ferguson	McCoist	Hateley	Huistra
Murray	Pressley	Brown	Steven	Ferguson	McSwegan	Hateley 2	Huistra
Murray	Pressley	Brown	Gordon	Ferguson	McSwegan 2	Hateley	Hagen
Gough	McPherson	Brown	Steven	Ferguson	McCoist	Durrant	Huistra
Other substitutes: Maxwell, Murray, Gordon							
Gough	McPherson	Brown	Murray	Ferguson	McSwegan	Hateley	Huistra
Gough	Kuznetsov	Brown	Gordon	Durrant	McSwegan	Hateley	Huistra
Gough	McPherson	Brown	Hagen	Ferguson	McSwegan	Durrant	Huistra
Gough	McPherson	Brown	Hagen	Ferguson	McSwegan	Durrant	Huistra
Gough	McPherson	Brown	Hagen	Ferguson	McSwegan	Durrant	Huistra
Murray	Gough	Brown	Ferguson	McCall	Durrant	Hateley	Huistra

Results 1993–94

DATE	OPPOSITION	VENUE	COMP	SCORE	CROWD	1	2	3
Aug 7	Hearts	H	PL	2-1	43,261	Maxwell	McCall	Wishart
Aug 11	Dumbarton	H	LC	1-0	36,309	Maxwell	Wishart	Vinnicom
Aug 14	St Johnstone	A	PL	2-1	10,152	Maxwell	Murray	Wishart
Aug 21	Celtic	A	PL	0-0	47,942	Maxwell	Pressley	Wishart
Aug 24	Dunfermline	A	LC	2-0	12,980	Maxwell	Wishart	D. Robert
Aug 28	Kilmarnock	H	PL	1-2	44,243	Maxwell	Stevens	D. Robert
Sep 1	Aberdeen	H	LC	2-1	45,604	Maxwell	Stevens	D. Robert
Sep 4	Dundee	A	PL	1-1	13,365	Maxwell	Stevens	D. Robert
Sep 11	Partick Thistle	H	PL	1-1	40,998	Maxwell	Stevens	D. Robert
Sep 15	Levski Sofia	H	EC	3-2	37,013	Maxwell	Stevens	D. Robert
Sep 18	Aberdeen	A	PL	0-2	20,000	Maxwell	Stevens	D. Robert
Sep 22	Celtic	H	LC	1-0	47,420	Maxwell	Stevens	D. Robert
Sep 25	Hibernian	H	PL	2-1	43,200	Maxwell	Stevens	D. Robert
Sep 29	Levski Sofia	A	EC	1-2	50,000	Maxwell	Stevens	Wishart
Oct 2	Raith Rovers	A	PL	1-1	8,500	Maxwell	Stevens	Murray
Oct 6	Motherwell	H	PL	1-2	39,816	Scott	Stevens	Murray
Oct 9	Dundee United	A	PL	3-1	11,045	Maxwell	Stevens	D. Robert
Oct 16	St Johnstone	H	PL	2-0	41,960	Maxwell	Stevens	D. Robert
Oct 24	Hibernian	Pkhd	LC	2-1	47,632	Maxwell	Stevens	D. Robert
Oct 30	Celtic	H	PL	1-2	47,522	Maxwell	Stevens	D. Robert
Nov 3	Hearts	A	PL	2-2	18,370	Maxwell	McCall	D. Robert
Nov 6	Kilmarnock	A	PL	2-0	19,162	Maxwell	McCall	D. Robert
Nov 10	Dundee United	H	PL	3-1	38,477	Maxwell	Stevens	D. Robert
Nov 13	Raith Rovers	H	PL	2-2	42,611	Maxwell	Stevens	D. Robert
Nov 20	Hibernian	A	PL	1-0	16,393	Maxwell	Murray	D. Robert
Nov 27	Partick Thistle	A	PL	1-1	17,292	Maxwell	McCall	D. Robert
Dec 1	Aberdeen	H	PL	2-0	45,182	Maxwell	McCall	D. Robert
Dec 4	Motherwell	A	PL	2-0	14,069	Maxwell	Stevens	D. Robert
Dec 11	Dundee United	H	PL	0-3	43,058	Maxwell	Stevens	D. Roberts
Dec 18	St Johnstone	A	PL	4-0	10,056	Maxwell	Stevens	Vinnicom
Dec 27	Hearts	H	PL	2-2	45,116	Maxwell	Stevens	Murray
Jan 1	Celtic	A	PL	4-2	48,506	Maxwell	Stevens	Murray
Jan 8	Kilmarnock	H	PL	3-0	44,919	Maxwell	Stevens	D. Robert
Jan 15	Dundee	A	PL	1-1	11,014	Maxwell	Stevens	D. Robert
Jan 22	Aberdeen	A	PL	0-0	21,500	Maxwell	Stevens	D. Roberts
Jan 29	Dumbarton	H	SC3	4-1	36,809	Maxwell	Stevens	D. Roberts
Feb 5	Partick Thistle	H	PL	5-1	42,606	Maxwell	Stevens	D. Robert
Feb 12	Hibernian	H	PL	2-0	43,265	Goram	Stevens	D. Roberts
Feb 19	Alloa	H	SC4	6-0	37,804	Goram	Stevens	D. Robert
Feb 26	Raith Rovers	A	PL	2-1	8,988	Goram	Stevens	D. Robert
Mar 5	Motherwell	H	PL	2-1	43,669	Goram	Stevens	D. Robert
Mar 12	Hearts	H	SCqf	2-0	41,666	Goram	McCall	D. Roberts
Mar 19	St Johnstone	H	PL	4-0	43,228	Goram	McCall	D. Roberts
Mar 26	Hearts	A	PL	2-1	18,108	Goram	Stevens	McCall
Mar 29	Partick Thistle	A	PL	2-1	12,000	Goram	Stevens	McCall
Apr 2	Aberdeen	H	PL	1-1	45,888	Goram	Stevens	Murray
Apr 5	Dundee United	A	PL	0-0	11,048	Goram	Moore	Murray
Apr 10	Kilmarnock	Hamp	SCsf	0-0	35,144	Maxwell	Murray	D. Roberts
Apr 10	Kilmarnock	Hamp	replay	2-1	29,860	Maxwell	McCall	D. Robert
Apr 16	Raith Rovers	H	PL	4-0	42,545	Maxwell	McCall	D. Robert
Apr 23	Dundee United	H	PL	2-1	44,776	Maxwell	McCall	D. Robert

4	5	6	7	8	9	10	11
Gough	Pressley	Brown	Murray	I. Ferguson	Hagen	Hateley	Mik'chenko
Gough	Pressley	Murray	Steven	I. Ferguson	Hagen	Hateley	Durrant
Gough	Pressley	Brown	Steven	I. Ferguson	Hagen	Durrant	Huistra
Gough	McPherson	Murray	Steven	I. Ferguson	D. Ferguson	Hateley	Huistra
Gough	Pressley	Durrant	Steven	I. Ferguson	D. Ferguson	Hateley	Mik'chenko
Gough	Pressley	Murray	Steven	I. Ferguson	D. Ferguson	Hateley	Mik'chenko
Gough	Pressley	Murray	Steven	I. Ferguson	Durrant	Hateley	Huistra
Gough	Pressley	Kuznetsov	Steven	I. Ferguson	D. Ferguson	Hateley	Huistra
Gough	McPherson	Vinnicombe	Steven	I. Ferguson	D. Ferguson	Hateley	Morrow
McCall	McPherson	Pressley	Steven	I. Ferguson	Durrant	Hateley 2	D. Ferguson

Other substitutes: Hagen, Morrow

4	5	6	7	8	9	10	11
McCall	McPherson	Pressley	Steven	I. Ferguson	Miller	Hateley	Huistra
Gough	McPherson	McCall	Steven	I. Ferguson	Durrant	Hateley	Huistra
Gough	McPherson	Wishart	Steven	I. Ferguson	Hagen	Hateley	Mik'chenko
Gough	McPherson	McCall	Steven	I. Ferguson	Durrant	Hateley	Hagen

Other substitutes: Murray, Dodds. Aggregate score 4-4. Levski Sofia win on away goals

4	5	6	7	8	9	10	11
Gough	Pressley	Durrant	Steven	I. Ferguson	McCoist	Hateley	Huistra
Gough	Pressley	Durrant	Steven	I. Ferguson	Hagen	Hateley	Morrow
Gough	McPherson	McCall	Mik'chenko	I. Ferguson	Durrant	Hateley	Huistra 2
Gough	McPherson	Mik'chenko	Steven	I. Ferguson	McCoist	Hateley	Huistra
Gough	McPherson	McCall	Steven	I. Ferguson	Durrant	Hateley	Huistra
Gough	McPherson	McCall	Steven	I. Ferguson	McCoist	Hateley	Durrant
Gough	McPherson	Brown	Mik'chenko	I. Ferguson	McCoist	Hateley 2	Huistra
Gough	McPherson	Brown	Mik'chenko	I. Ferguson	McCoist	Hateley	Durrant
McCall	McPherson	Brown	Durrant	I. Ferguson	McCoist 2	Hateley	Mik'chenko
Gough	McCall	Brown	Mik'chenko	I. Ferguson	Durrant	Hateley 2	Huistra
Gough	McPherson	Brown	McCall	I. Ferguson	Durrant	Hateley	Mik'chenko
Gough	McPherson	Brown	Durie	I. Ferguson	Durrant	Hateley	Mik'chenko
Gough	McPherson	Brown	Steven	I. Ferguson	Durie	Hateley 2	Murray
McCall	McPherson	Pressley	Steven	I. Ferguson	Durie 2	Hateley	Murray
Gough	McPherson	McCall	Steven	I. Ferguson	Durie	Hateley	Murray
McCall	Pressley	Kuznetsov	Steven	Murray	Durie	Hateley 2	Mik'chenko
McCall	Pressley	Brown	Steven	Kuznetsov	Durie	Hateley 2	Mik'chenko
Gough	Pressley	Brown	Steven	McCall	Durie	Hateley	Mik'chenko 2
Gough	Murray	Brown	Steven	McCall	Durie	Hateley 2	Mik'chenko
Murray	Pressley	Brown	Steven	McCall	Durie	Hateley	Mik'chenko
Gough	Murray	Brown	Steven	McCall	Durie	Hateley	Mik'chenko
Gough	Murray	Brown	Steven	McCall	Durie	Hateley	Mik'chenko
Gough	Murray	Brown	Steven	McCall	Durie 2	Hateley	Mik'chenko
Gough	McCall	Brown	Steven	I. Ferguson	Durie	Hateley	Mik'chenko
McCall	McPherson	Brown	Steven	I. Ferguson	McCoist 3	Hateley	Mik'chenko
McCall	McPherson	Brown	Steven	I. Ferguson	McCoist	Hateley	Durie
Gough	McCall	Brown	Steven	I. Ferguson	Durie	Hateley	Mik'chenko
Gough	McPherson	Brown	Steven	I. Ferguson	McCoist	Hateley	Durie
Gough	McPherson	Brown	Steven	I. Ferguson	McCoist	Hateley	Durie
Gough	McPherson	Brown	Steven	I. Ferguson	McCoist	Hateley	Durie
Gough	McPherson	Brown	Steven	I. Ferguson	McCoist	Hateley	Mik'chenko
Gough	McPherson	Brown	McCall	I. Ferguson	McCoist	Hateley	Durie
Gough	McPherson	Pressley	McCall	Durrant	Durie	D. Ferguson	Mik'chenko
Gough	McPherson	Brown	McCall	I. Ferguson	Durie	Hateley	Mik'chenko
Gough	McPherson	Pressley	Durie	I. Ferguson	McCoist	Hateley 2	Durrant
Gough	McPherson	Brown	Durrant	I. Ferguson	McCoist	D. Ferguson	Durie
Gough	McPherson	Brown	Steven	I. Ferguson	McCoist	Hateley	Durie 2

Andy Goram

Results 1993–94 *Continued*

DATE	OPPOSITION	VENUE	COMP	SCORE	CROWD	1	2	3
Apr 26	Motherwell	A	PL	1-2	14,050	Maxwell	McCall	D. Robertso
Apr 30	Celtic	H	PL	1-1	45,853	Scott	McCall	D. Robertso
May 3	Hibernian	A	PL	0-1	14,517	Scott	McCall	D. Robertso
May 7	Kilmarnock	A	PL	0-1	18,012	Scott	Wishart	D. Robertso
May 14	Dundee United	H	PL			Scott		
May 21	Scot Cup Final					Maxwell		

4	5	6	7	8	9	10	11
Gough	McPherson	Pressley	Steven	I. Ferguson	McCoist	D. Ferguson	Durie
Gough	McPherson	Pressley	Steven	I. Ferguson	McCoist	Hateley	Durie
Gough	McPherson	Pressley	Steven	I. Ferguson	Durrant	Hateley	Mik'chenko
Gough	Murray	Kuznetsov	Durrant	Miller	McCoist	Hateley	Mik'chenko

Andy Goram

Results 1994–95

DATE	OPPOSITION	VENUE	COMP	SCORE	CROWD	1	2	3
Aug 5	Sampdoria	H	F	2-4	27,282	Goram	McCall	D. Roberts
Aug 6	Man United	H	F	1-0	30,186	Maxwell	Stevens	Murray
Aug 10	AEK Athens	A	EC	0-2	30,000	Goram	Stevens	D. Roberts
Aug 13	Motherwell	H	PL	2-1	43,750	Goram	Murray	D. Roberts
Aug 17	Arbroath	A	CC	6-1	4,665	Maxwell	McCall	Brown
Aug 20	Partick Thistle	A	PL	2-0	15,030	Goram	McCall	Brown
Aug 24	AEK Athens	H	EC	0-1	44,789	Goram	McCall	D. Roberts
Aug 27	Celtic	H	PL	0-2	45,466	Goram	McCall	Pressley
Aug 31	Falkirk	H	CC	1-2	40,697	Goram	McCall	D. Roberts
Sep 11	Hearts	H	PL	3-0	41,041	Goram	McCall	D. Roberts
Sep 17	Falkirk	A	PL	2-0	12,500	Goram	McCall	D. Roberts
Sep 24	Aberdeen	A	PL	2-2	21,000	Goram	Moore	D. Roberts
Oct 1	Dundee United	H	PL	2-0	43,030	Goram	Moore	D. Roberts
Oct 8	Hibernian	A	PL	1-2	12,118	Goram	Moore	D. Roberts
Oct 15	Kilmarnock	H	PL	2-0	44,099	Goram	Moore	D. Roberts
Oct 22	Motherwell	A	PL	1-2	11,160	Goram	Moore	D. Roberts
Oct 30	Celtic	A	PL	3-1	32,171	Goram	Wishart	D. Roberts
Nov 5	Partick Thistle	H	PL	3-0	43,696	Goram	Wishart	D. Roberts
Nov 9	Hearts	A	PL	1-1	12,347	Goram	Moore	D. Roberts
Nov 19	Falkirk	H	PL	1-1	44,018	Goram	Moore	D. Roberts
Nov 25	Aberdeen	H	PL	1-0	45,072	Goram	Wishart	D. Roberts
Dec 4	Dundee United	A	PL	3-0	10,692	Goram	McCall	D. Roberts
Dec 10	Kilmarnock	A	PL	2-1	17,283	Goram	McCall	D. Roberts
Dec 26	Hibernian	H	PL	2-0	44,892	Scott	McCall	D. Roberts
Dec 31	Motherwell	A	PL	3-1	11,500	Scott	McCall	D. Roberts
Jan 4	Celtic	H	PL	1-1	45,794	Scott	McCall	D. Roberts
Jan 7	Partick Thistle	A	PL	1-1	19,351	Goram	Moore	D. Roberts
Jan 14	Falkirk	A	PL	3-2	13,495	Maxwell	Moore	D. Roberts
Jan 21	Hearts	H	PL	1-0	44,231	Maxwell	McCall	Brown
Feb 4	Dundee United	H	PL	1-1	44,197	Maxwell	Moore	D. Roberts
Feb 6	Hamilton Accies	A	SC3	3-1	18,379	Maxwell	Moore	D. Roberts
Feb 12	Aberdeen	A	PL	0-2	20,000	Maxwell	Moore	D. Roberts
Feb 20	Hearts	A	SC4	2-4	12,375	Maxwell	Moore	D. Roberts
Feb 25	Kilmarnock	H	PL	3-0	44,859	Maxwell	McCall	D. Roberts
Mar 4	Hibernian	A	PL	1-1	12,059	Maxwell	Moore	Bollan
Mar 11	Falkirk	H	PL	2-2	43,359	Maxwell	McCall	Bollan
Mar 18	Hearts	A	PL	1-2	9,806	Maxwell	Cleland	Bollan
Apr 1	Dundee United	A	PL	2-0	11,500	Thomson	Cleland	Brown
Apr 8	Aberdeen	H	PL	3-2	44,460	Thomson	Cleland	Brown
Apr 16	Hibernian	H	PL	3-1	44,193	Thomson	Cleland	Brown
Apr 20	Kilmarnock	A	PL	1-0	16,086	Maxwell	Moore	Bollan
Apr 29	Motherwell	H	PL	0-2	43,576	Thomson	Cleland	Mik'chen
May 7	Celtic	A	PL	0-3	31,025	Thomson	Moore	Cleland
May 13	Partick Thistle	H	PL			Maxwell		

4	5	6	7	8	9	10	11
Gough	McPherson	Brown	Steven	I. Ferguson	McCoist	Hateley	Laudrup
Other substitutes: Durie, Murray							
Boli	Pressley	Moore	Durrant	Durie	McCoist	D. Ferguson	Huistra
Other substitutes: Gough, Reid							
Gough	Pressley	McCall	Laudrup	I. Ferguson	Durie	Hateley	Murray
Other substitutes: McPherson, McCoist							
Gough	Boli	McPherson	Durrant	McCall	McCoist	Hateley	Laudrup
Gough	Boli	McPherson	Moore	I. Ferguson	D. Ferguson 3	Hateley 2	Durrant
Gough	Boli	McPherson	Moore	I. Ferguson	D. Ferguson	Hateley	Laudrup
Gough	Boli	McPherson	Durie	I. Ferguson	D. Ferguson	Hateley	Laudrup
Other substitutes: Murray, Hagen							
Gough	Boli	McPherson	Durrant	I. Ferguson	Durie	Hateley	Laudrup
Gough	McPherson	Moore	Durrant	I. Ferguson	Durie	Hateley	Laudrup
Gough	McPherson	Moore	Murray	I. Ferguson	Durrant	Hateley 2	Laudrup
Gough	Moore	Boli	Durie	I. Ferguson	Durrant	Hateley	Laudrup
Gough	McPherson	Boli	Murray	McCall	Durie	Hateley	Laudrup
Gough	McPherson	Boli	McCall	Mik'chenko	Miller	Hateley	Laudrup
Gough	McPherson	Boli	McCall	Huistra	Miller	Hateley	Laudrup
McCall	McPherson	Pressley	Murray	Huistra	Miller	Hateley	Laudrup
McCall	McPherson	Boli	Murray	Huistra	Miller	Hateley	Laudrup
McCall	McLaren	Boli	Huistra	Murray	Miller	Hateley 2	Laudrup
McCall	McLaren	Boli	Huistra	Murray	Miller	Hateley	Laudrup
McCall	McLaren	Boli	Huistra	Murray	Durrant	Hateley	Laudrup
McCall	McLaren	Boli	Huistra	Miller	McCoist	Hateley	Laudrup
McCall	McLaren	Boli	Huistra	Miller	McCoist	Hateley	Laudrup
Gough	McLaren	Boli	Huistra	Miller	McCoist	Durie	Laudrup
Gough	McLaren	Murray	Huistra	Miller	Durie	Durrant	Laudrup
Gough	McLaren	Boli	Huistra	Miller	Durie	Hateley	Laudrup
Gough	McLaren	Boli	Huistra	Miller	Durie	Moore	Laudrup
Gough	McLaren	Boli	Huistra	I. Ferguson	Durie	Miller	Laudrup
McCall	McLaren	Brown	Huistra	I. Ferguson	Durrant	McGinty	Murray
McCall	McLaren	Brown	Huistra 2	I. Ferguson	Miller	Murray	Durrant
Gough	McLaren	Boli	Steven	I. Ferguson	Miller	Murray	Laudrup
Gough	Boli	McCall	Steven	Miller	Durie	Hateley	Laudrup
Gough	Boli	McCall	Steven	Miller	Durie	Hateley	Laudrup
Gough	Boli	Bollan	Cleland	McCall	Miller	Hateley	Laudrup
Gough	McLaren	Cleland	Steven	McCall	Miller	Durie	Laudrup
Gough	McLaren	Boli	Steven	Cleland	Miller	Durie	Laudrup
Gough	McLaren	Boli	Steven	Murray	Durie	McCall	Brown
Gough	McLaren	Boli	Durrant	I. Ferguson	Durie	Brown	Laudrup
Gough	McLaren	Boli	Steven	I. Ferguson	Durie	McCall	Laudrup
Gough	McLaren	Boli	McCall	Miller	Durie	Durrant	Laudrup
Gough	McLaren	Boli	Steven	Miller	Durrant	Hateley	Laudrup
Gough	McLaren	Durrant	Steven	Miller	Durie	Hateley	Laudrup
Gough	McLaren	Murray	Cleland	I. Ferguson	Durrant	Mik'chenko	Laudrup
Gough	McLaren	Boli	Steven	I. Ferguson	Durrant	Hateley	Laudrup
Boli	McLaren	Brown	Steven	I. Ferguson	Durrant	Hateley	Laudrup

Andy Goram

Results 1995–96

DATE	OPPOSITION	VENUE	COMP	SCORE	CROWD	1	2	3
Aug 9	A. Famagusta	H	EC	1-0	43,519	Goram	Wright	D. Roberts•
Aug 19	Morton	H	CC2	3-0	42,941	Goram	Wright	D. Roberts•
Aug 23	A. Famagusta	A	EC	0-0	9,500	Goram	Wright	D. Roberts•
Aug 26	Kilmarnock	H	PL	1-0	44,686	Goram	Wright	D. Roberts•
Aug 30	Stirling Albion	H	CC3	3-2	36,685	Goram	Wright	D. Roberts•
Sep 9	Raith Rovers	H	PL	4-0	43,535	Goram	Wright	D. Roberts•
Sep 13	Steaua Bucharest	A	EC	0-1	26,000	Goram	Wright	Cleland
Sep 16	Falkirk	A	PL	2-0	11,445	Goram	Moore	D. Roberts•
Sep 20	Celtic	A	CC4	1-0	32,789	Goram	Wright	D. Roberts•
Sep 23	Hibernian	H	PL	0-1	44,364	Goram	Wright	Cleland
Sep 27	Borussia Dortmund	H	EC	2-2	33,209	Goram	Wright	Cleland
Sep 30	Celtic	A	PL	2-0	34,500	Goram	Wright	Cleland
Oct 3	Motherwell	H	PL	2-1	37,348	Goram	Moore	Cleland
Oct 7	Aberdeen	A	PL	1-0	22,500	Goram	Wright	D. Roberts•
Oct 14	Partick Thistle	A	PL	4-0	16,346	Goram	Wright	D. Roberts•
Oct 18	Juventus	A	EC	1-4	50,000	Goram	Wright	D. Roberts•
Oct 21	Hearts	H	PL	4-1	45,155	Goram	Moore	D. Roberts•
Oct 24	Aberdeen	Hamp	CC5	1-2	26,131	Goram	Wright	Brown
Oct 28	Raith Rovers	A	PL	2-2	9,200	Goram	Moore	Cleland
Nov 1	Juventus	H	EC	0-4	42,523	Goram	Wright	Bollan
Nov 4	Falkirk	H	PL	2-0	42,059	Scott	Cleland	Bollan
Nov 8	Kilmarnock	A	PL	2-0	14,823	Scott	Cleland	Bollan
Nov 11	Aberdeen	H	PL	1-1	45,427	Thomson	Cleland	Bollan
Nov 19	Celtic	H	PL	3-3	46,640	Goram	Cleland	D. Robertsc
Nov 22	Steaua Bucharest	H	EC	1-1	30,800	Goram	Brown	D. Roberts•
Nov 25	Hibernian	A	PL	4-1	13,558	Goram	Cleland	Bollan
Dec 2	Hearts	A	PL	2-0	15,105	Goram	Cleland	D. Roberts•
Dec 6	Borussia Dortmund	A	EC	2-2	35,800	Goram	Cleland	D. Robertsc
Dec 9	Partick Thistle	H	PL	1-0	43,173	Goram	Moore	D. Robertsc
Dec 19	Motherwell	A	PL	0-0	10,197	Goram	McInnes	D. Roberts•
Dec 26	Kilmarnock	H	PL	3-0	45,173	Goram	Ferguson	D. Robertsc
Dec 30	Hibernian	H	PL	7-0	44,692	Goram	Ferguson	D. Robertsc
Jan 3	Celtic	A	PL	0-0	37,000	Goram	Ferguson	D. Robertsc
Jan 6	Falkirk	A	PL	4-0	10,581	Goram	Ferguson	D. Robertsc
Jan 13	Raith Rovers	H	PL	4-0	42,498	Goram	Ferguson	D. Roberts•
Jan 20	Hearts	H	PL	0-3	45,096	Goram	Ferguson	D. Robertsc
Jan 27	Keith	A	SC3	10-1	14,000	Goram	Cleland 3	D. Robertsc
Feb 3	Partick Thistle	A	PL	2-1	16,523	Goram	Cleland	D. Robertsc
Feb 10	Motherwell	H	PL	3-2	45,566	Goram	Ferguson	D. Robertsc
Feb 15	Clyde	A	SC4	4-1	5,722	Goram	Ferguson	D. Robertsc
Feb 25	Aberdeen	A	PL	1-0	21,000	Goram	Moore	D. Robertsc
Mar 3	Hibernian	A	PL	2-0	11,954	Goram	Moore	D. Robertsc
Mar 9	Caledonian Thistle	A	SC5	3-0	12,000	Goram	Moore	D. Robertsc
Mar 17	Celtic	H	PL	1-1	47,312	Goram	Moore	Cleland
Mar 23	Falkirk	H	PL	3-2	46,014	Scott	Miller	Cleland

4	5	6	7	8	9	10	11
Gough	McLaren	Reid	McCall	Gascoigne	Ferguson	Hateley	Laudrup
Other substitutes: Durie, Miller							
Gough	Moore	Ferguson	Miller	Gascoigne	McCoist	Hateley	Mik'chenko
Gough	McLaren	Petric	McCall	Gascoigne	Miller	Hateley	Durie
Other substitutes: Cleland, Murray							
Gough	McLaren	Petric	Steven	Miller	McCoist	McCall	Durie
Gough	McLaren	Petric	McCall	Miller	McCoist	Hateley	Mik'chenko
Gough	McLaren	Petric	Miller	Gascoigne	McCoist 2	Salenko	Laudrup
Gough	McLaren	Petric	Miller	Gascoigne	McCoist	Durrant	Laudrup
Other substitutes: Bollan, Reid							
Gough	McLaren	Petric	Murray	Durie	Salenko	Miller	Mik'chenko
Gough	McLaren	Petric	Miller	Gascoigne	McCoist	Salenko	Laudrup
Gough	McLaren	Petric	Miller	Gascoigne	McCoist	Salenko	Laudrup
Gough	McCall	Petric	Miller	Gascoigne	McCoist	Durie	Laudrup
Other substitutes: Murray, Brown							
Gough	McLaren	Petric	McCall	Gascoigne	McCoist	Salenko	Ferguson
Gough	McLaren	Petric	Durie	Gascoigne	McCoist	Ferguson	Mik'chenko
Gough	McLaren	Petric	Cleland	Durrant	Salenko	McCall	Durie
Gough	McLaren	Petric	Cleland	Durrant	Durrie 3	McCall	Mik'chenko
Gough	Moore	Petric	Durie	McCall	McCoist	Salenko	Cleland
Other substitutes: Murray, Bollan							
Gough	McLaren	Petric	Cleland	Gascoigne	Salenko 2	Durie	Mik'chenko
Moore	McLaren	Petric	Cleland	Gascoigne	McCoist	Salenko	Durie
Gough	McLaren	Petric	Murray	Gascoigne	McCoist	Salenko	Durie
Gough	Brown	Petric	Ferguson	Gascoigne	Miller	Salenko	McCall
Other substitutes: Murray, Reid							
Gough	McLaren	Petric	Durrant	Ferguson	McCoist 2	McCall	Durie
Gough	McLaren	Petric	Durrant	Gascoigne	McCoist	Salenko	Ferguson
Gough	McLaren	Petric	Ferguson	Gascoigne	Salenko	McCall	Mik'chenko
Gough	McLaren	Petric	Ferguson	Gascoigne	Salenko	McCall	Laudrup
Gough	McLaren	Petric	Durrant	Gascoigne	McCoist	McCall	Laudrup
Other substitutes: Boyack, Scott							
Gough	McLaren	Petric	Miller	Gascoigne	McCoist	Salenko	McGinty
Gough	McLaren	Petric	McGinty	Gascoigne	McCoist	Miller	Laudrup
Gough	McLaren	Bollan	Miller	Gascoigne	Durie	McCall	Laudrup
Other substitutes: McGinty, Scott							
Gough	McLaren	Petric	Miller	McInnes	McCoist	Durie	Laudrup
Gough	McLaren	Petric	Mik'chenko	Ferguson	Miller	Durie	Laudrup
Gough	McLaren	Petric	Miller	Gascoigne	Salenko	Durie	Laudrup
Gough	McLaren	Petric	Miller	Gascoigne	Salenko	Durie 4	Laudrup
Gough	McLaren	Petric	Miller	Gascoigne	Salenko	Durie	Laudrup
Gough	McLaren	Petric	Cleland	Gascoigne	McCoist 2	Durie	McInnes
Gough	McLaren	Petric	McInnes	Gascoigne	McCoist	Durie 2	Laudrup
Gough	McLaren	Petric	Miller	Cleland	Durrant	Durie	Laudrup
Gough	McLaren	Petric	Ferguson 3	McCall	Miller	Durie	Laudrup
Brown	McLaren	Petric	Van Vossen	Gascoigne 2	Miller	McCall	Laudrup
Moore	McLaren	Petric	Miller	Gascoigne	Van Vossen	McCall	Laudrup
Moore	McLaren	Petric	Miller 2	Gascoigne	Van Vossen	McCall	Laudrup
Petric	McLaren	Brown	Miller	Gascoigne	Ferguson	McCall	Laudrup
Gough	McLaren	Petric	Van Vossen	Gascoigne	Andersen	McCall	Laudrup
Petric	McLaren	Brown	Van Vossen	Gascoigne 2	McCoist	Miller	Laudrup
Petric	McLaren	Brown	Miller	Gascoigne	McCoist	McCall	Laudrup
Petric	McLaren	Brown	Andersen 2	Gascoigne	McCoist	McCall	Laudrup

Results 1995–96 *Continued*

DATE	OPPOSITION	VENUE	COMP	SCORE	CROWD	1	2	3
Mar 30	Raith Rovers	A	PL	4-2	9,300	Snelders	Petric	Cleland
Apr 7	Celtic	Hamp	SCsf	2-1	36,333	Goram	Cleland	D. Robert
Apr 10	Hearts	A	PL	0-2	15,350	Goram	Cleland	D. Robert
Apr 13	Partick Thistle	H	PL	5-0	46,438	Goram	Cleland	D. Robert
Apr 20	Motherwell	A	PL	3-1	13,128	Goram	Steven	D. Robert
Apr 28	Aberdeen	H	PL			Goram	Steven	D. Robert
May 4	Kilmarnock	A	PL			Snelders	Steven	D. Robert
May 18	Hearts	Hamp	SCf			Goram	Cleland	D. Robert

4	5	6	7	8	9	10	11
Durie	McLaren	Brown	Andersen	Gascoigne	McCoist 3	McCall	Laudrup
Petric	McLaren	Brown	Durie	Gascoigne	McCoist	McCall	Laudrup
Gough	McLaren	Petric	Steven	Gascoigne	McCoist	McCall	Laudrup
Gough	McLaren	Brown	Durie	Gascoigne	Andersen 3	McCall	Laudrup
Gough	McLaren	Brown	Durie	Gascoigne	Andersen	McCall	Laudrup
Gough	McLaren	Brown	Durie	Gascoigne	Andersen	McCall	Laudrup
Gough	McLaren	Brown	Durie	Gascoigne	Andersen	McCall	Laudrup
Gough	McLaren	Brown	Durie	Gascoigne	Ferguson	McCall	Laudrup

Andy Goram

Results 1996–97

DATE	OPPOSITION	VENUE	COMP	SCORE	CROWD	1	2	3
Aug 7	Alania Vladikavkaz	H	EC	3-1	44,799	Goram	Cleland	Albertz
Aug 10	Raith Rovers	H	PL	1-0	46,221	Goram	Steven	Albertz
Aug 14	Clydebank	A	CC2	3-0	7,450	Goram	Wright	Albertz
Aug 17	Dunfermline	A	PL	5-2	16,495	Goram	Cleland	Albertz
Aug 21	Alania Vladikavkaz	A	EC	7-2	32,000	Goram	Cleland	Albertz
Aug 24	Dundee United	H	PL	1-0	48,285	Goram	Cleland	Albertz
Sep 4	Ayr United	H	CC3	3-1	44,282	Goram	Cleland	Albertz
Sep 7	Motherwell	A	PL	1-0	12,288	Goram	Cleland	Albertz
Sep 11	Grasshopper	A	EC	0-3	20,030	Goram	Cleland	Albertz
Sep 14	Hearts	H	PL	3-0	47,240	Goram	Cleland	Albertz
Sep 18	Hibernian	H	CC4	4-0	45,104	Goram	Moore	Albertz
Sep 21	Kilmarnock	A	PL	4-1	14,812	Goram	Moore	Albertz
Sep 25	Auxerre	H	EC	1-2	37,344	Goram	Cleland	Albertz
Sep 28	Celtic	H	PL	2-0	50,124	Goram	Moore	Albertz
Oct 12	Hibernian	A	PL	1-2	12,864	Goram	Moore	Albertz
Oct 16	Ajax	A	EC	1-4	47,000	Snelders	Cleland	Albertz
Oct 19	Aberdeen	H	PL	2-2	50,076	Snelders	Shields	Albertz
Oct 22	Dunfermline	N	CCsf	6-1	16,791	Snelders	Cleland	D. Robertson
Oct 26	Motherwell	H	PL	5-0	48,160	Snelders	Moore	Cleland
Oct 30	Ajax	H	EC	0-1	42,265	Snelders	Shields	Albertz
Nov 2	Raith Rovers	A	PL	2-2	9,705	Snelders	Cleland	D. Robertson
Nov 14	Celtic	A	PL	1-0	50,041	Goram	Cleland	D. Robertson
Nov 20	Grasshopper	H	EC	2-1	34,192	Goram	Cleland	D. Robertson
Nov 24	Hearts	N	CCf	4-3	48,559	Goram	Cleland	Moore
Dec 1	Aberdeen	A	PL	3-0	21,500	Goram	Shields	D. Robertson
Dec 4	Auxerre	A	EC	1-2	21,000	Goram	Shields	D. Robertson
Dec 7	Hibernian	H	PL	4-3	48,053	Goram	Shields	D. Robertson
Dec 10	Dundee United	A	PL	0-1	12,529	Goram	Cleland	D. Robertson
Dec 14	Dunfermline	H	PL	3-1	45,878	Goram	Cleland	D. Robertson
Dec 17	Kilmarnock	H	PL	4-2	39,469	Goram	Cleland	D. Robertson
Dec 21	Hearts	A	PL	4-1	15,139	Goram	Cleland	D. Robertson
Dec 26	Raith Rovers	H	PL	4-0	48,322	Goram	Cleland	D. Robertson
Jan 2	Celtic	H	PL	3-1	50,019	Goram	Cleland	D. Robertson
Jan 4	Hibernian	A	PL	2-1	12,557	Snelders	Cleland	D. Robertson
Jan 12	Aberdeen	H	PL	4-0	47,509	Goram	Cleland	D. Robertson
Jan 15	Kilmarnock	A	PL	1-1	16,432	Goram	Cleland	Moore
Jan 18	Motherwell	A	PL	3-1	13,166	Goram	Cleland	D. Robertson
Jan 25	St Johnstone	H	SC3	2-0	44,989	Goram	Cleland	D. Robertson
Feb 1	Hearts	H	PL	0-0	50,024	Goram	Cleland	D. Robertson
Feb 8	Dunfermline	A	PL	3-0	15,840	Goram	Cleland	D. Robertson
Feb 15	East Fife	H	SC4	3-0	41,064	Goram	Cleland	D. Robertson
Feb 23	Hibernian	H	PL	3-1	47,618	Goram	Cleland	D. Robertson
Mar 1	Aberdeen	A	PL	2-2	16,331	Goram	Cleland	D. Robertson
Mar 6	Celtic	A	SC5	0-2	49,519	Goram	Cleland	D. Robertson
Mar 12	Dundee United	H	PL	0-2	49,192	Goram	Cleland	Moore

Due to injury, Andy Goram did not play in the final seven matches of the 1996–97 season

4	5	6	7	8	9	10	11
Gough	Petric	Bjorklund	McCall	Ferguson	McCoist	Durie	Laudrup

Other substitutes: McInnes, Snelders

4	5	6	7	8	9	10	11
Gough	Petric	Bjorklund	Durie	McInnes	McCoist	McCall	Laudrup
Gough	Petric	Shields	Durrant	McInnes	Miller	McCall	Van Vossen 2
Gough	Petric	Bjorklund	Van Vossen 2	Miller	McCoist 3	McCall	Laudrup
Gough	Petric	Bjorklund	McCall	McInnes	McCoist 3	Van Vossen	Laudrup 2

Other substitutes: Shields, Snelders

4	5	6	7	8	9	10	11
Gough	Petric	Bjorklund	Miller	Gascoigne	McCoist	McCall	Laudrup
Gough	Petric	Bjorklund	Durie	Gascoigne	Durrant	Miller	Van Vossen
Gough	Petric	Bjorklund	Durie	Gascoigne	McInnes	McCall	Laudrup
Gough	Petric	Bjorklund	McCall	Gascoigne	McCoist	Durie	Laudrup

Other substitutes: Moore, Snelders

4	5	6	7	8	9	10	11
Gough	Petric	Bjorklund	McCall	Gascoigne	McInnes	Durie	Laudrup
Gough	Petric	Bjorklund	Durie	Gascoigne	McCoist	McCall	Cleland
Gough	Petric	Bjorklund	Durie	Gascoigne 2	Cleland	McCall	Laudrup
Gough	Moore	Bjorklund	Van Vossen	Gascoigne	McInnes	Durie	Laudrup

Other substitutes: Andersen, Ferguson

4	5	6	7	8	9	10	11
Gough	Petric	Bjorklund	Cleland	Gascoigne	Van Vossen	McCall	Laudrup
Gough	Petric	Bjorklund	Cleland	Gascoigne	Van Vossen	Ferguson	Laudrup
Gough	Moore	Bjorklund	McCall	Gascoigne	Ferguson	McInnes	Laudrup

Other substitutes: Petric, Rae

4	5	6	7	8	9	10	11
Gough	Moore	Bjorklund	Van Vossen	Gascoigne	Miller	Cleland	Laudrup
Gough	Petric	Bjorklund	McInnes	Gascoigne	Andersen 2	Albertz	Laudrup 2
Gough	Petric	Bjorklund	McInnes	Gascoigne 3	Andersen	Albertz	Laudrup 2
Wilson	Petric	Bjorklund	D. Robertson	Durrant	Miller	McInnes	Laudrup

Other substitutes: McGinty, Rae

4	5	6	7	8	9	10	11
Gough	Petric	Bjorklund	Durrant	Gascoigne	McCoist	Albertz	Van Vossen
Gough	Petric	Bjorklund	Moore	Gascoigne	McInnes	Albertz	Laudrup
Gough	Petric	Wilson	Moore	Miller	McCoist 2	Albertz	Van Vossen

Other substitutes: Shields, Snelders

4	5	6	7	8	9	10	11
Gough	Petric	Bjorklund	Miller	Gascoigne 2	McCoist 2	Albertz	Laudrup
Gough	Petric	Bjorklund	Moore	Gascoigne	McCoist	Albertz	Laudrup
Gough	Petric	Moore	Steven	McInnes	Andersen	Ferguson	Van Vossen

Other substitutes: Nicolson, Snelders

4	5	6	7	8	9	10	11
Gough	Wilson	Moore	McInnes	Gascoigne	McCoist 2	Ferguson	Laudrup
Gough	Petric	Moore	McInnes	Gascoigne	McCoist	Ferguson	Laudrup
Gough	Petric	Moore	Steven	Gascoigne	McCoist	Ferguson	Laudrup
Gough	McLaren	Ferguson	Steven	Gascoigne	Andersen 3	Albertz	Laudrup
Gough	McLaren	Ferguson	Steven	Gascoigne	Andersen	Albertz	Laudrup
Gough	McLaren	Ferguson	Miller	Gascoigne	McCoist	Albertz	Laudrup
Petric	McLaren	Bjorklund	Moore	Gascoigne	McCoist	Albertz	Ferguson
Shields	Petric	Moore	McInnes	Ferguson	Andersen	Albertz	Laudrup
Gough	McLaren	Bjorklund	McInnes	Gascoigne	Andersen 2	Albertz	Laudrup
Gough	Petric	Bjorklund	Ferguson	Gascoigne	McCoist	Albertz	Laudrup
Gough	McLaren	Moore	Ferguson	Gascoigne	Andersen	Albertz	Laudrup
Gough	McLaren	Moore	Ferguson	Gascoigne	Andersen	Albertz	Rozental
Gough	McLaren	Bjorklund	Durie	McInnes	McCoist	Ferguson	Laudrup
Gough	McLaren	Bjorklund	Durie	Ferguson	Moore	Albertz	Laudrup
Gough	Steven	Bjorklund	Durie	Ferguson	McCoist	Albertz	Laudrup
Gough	McLaren	Bjorklund	Steven	Ferguson	Durie	Albertz	Laudrup
Petric	McLaren	Bjorklund	Moore	Ferguson	Durie	Albertz	Laudrup
Petric	McLaren	Bjorklund	Moore	Ferguson	Andersen	Albertz	Laudrup
Petric	McLaren	Bjorklund	Durie	Ferguson	Miller	Albertz	Laudrup